BADASS
BACKYARD
COOKING

JOHAN MAGNUSSON
BIG SWEDE BBQ

BADASS BACKYARD COOKING

140 OF MY FAVORITE OUTDOOR COOKING RECIPES

TO MY WONDERFUL WIFE, YOU INSPIRE ME EVERY DAY.

First published in the USA in 2021 by
Magnusson Partners Incorporated dba Big Swede BBQ
5527 E Beck Lane
Scottsdale AZ, 85254
www.BigSwedeBBQ.com

ISBN: 978-0-578-99358-4

Library of Congress Control Number: 2021919008

Cover Design by Johan Magnusson
Book Design by Johan Magnusson
Book layout by Johan Magnusson
Editing by Connie Dowell
Photography by Johan Magnusson
Additional photography by Burk Forsythe and Brett Edwards

Printed and bound in the United States.

CONTENTS

BIG SWEDE BBQ BADASS RECIPE COLLECTION

ABOUT THIS BOOK

I am not a trained chef, nor do I own a restaurant.

I am just a regular guy with a burning passion for cooking food outdoors.

I love to help people cook better food and utilize their backyards and their outdoor cooking equipment a little more. I am blown away when I see what people have installed in their backyards when it comes to grills, smokers and other cooking tools. I am equally surprised when I learn that they only use these tools once in a while when they grill up some burgers, steaks, or hot dogs.

I hope this cookbook can help with that. Everything you can cook indoors, you can cook outdoors. And you won't set off the smoke alarm either.

This cookbook is a collection of 140 recipes that I love to cook in my own backyard. And when I create recipes, I try to follow these three guidelines:

1. It should taste Badass!
2. It should be easy to make.
3. It should also be fun and something different.

This cookbook does not have tons and tons of pages with recipes for rubs and sauces. Being in the BBQ industry for a while now, I have realized that there are plenty of people out there, people like myself, that invest their lives and spend endless hours blending and test cooking rubs, sauces, glazes, and marinades. They literally cook 100 versions of the same dish to get the balance of a rub or a sauce perfect before they sell their products commercially. My recommendation to everyone I meet, don't waste your time blending your own rubs – buy it from folks that do this for a living.

In this book, I will recommend which of our Badass BBQ Boosts that would work great for a specific dish, but you can just as easily exchange one of our seasonings with something else that you like. I even recommend people to mix different rubs together to create their own favorite flavor profile. That is what I love about cooking and grilling, there is never one way or the "correct way" of doing things. Have fun with it and experiment!

I also won't bore you with explanations of my food philosophy or pages filled with BBQ 101 stuff, like how to light a grill. Or which fuel to use and when. Or what kind of different cookers are out there. If you want to read about that, this is not the book for you. If you want to know a little bit about myself and Big Swede BBQ got started, I have included some pages at the end of this book.

This book is all about food inspiration, recipes and more recipes. It is about the joy of cooking outside with friends and family. It is about the love of heat, fire and smoke.

But enough of this, turn the page and start cooking!!

Happy Grilling!!

OUR BADASS RECIPES

APPET

Appetizers

A great appetizer sets the stage for the rest of the dinner. It is the attention grabber. It is the dish that gets people excited for the next course. Truth to be told, sometimes the appetizers are the best dishes of the entire meal. And it is often the dish that allows us to get a little bit creative in our outdoor kitchens.

Almost any thing goes as an appetizer if it is served in small portions. Soup is a great appetizer. But so is a fun sallad. And what about bitesize baconwrapped brisket slices? Flatbread is like a pizza appetizer. The best appetizer I think I ever made was a thanksgiving appetizer where we cooked turkey breast in small chunks and served them skewered together with a cranberry jelly cube and fried stuffing balls on a pipette filled with flavorful gravy. Our guests were blown away by this dish.

I like appetizers like that. Appetizers that surprises my guests – there should be an element of joy when eating them. But I also believe that a great appetizer should be easy to make and not be overly complicated to put together. So I have included recipes in this section that have an element of fun to them, but that are also rather simple to cook.

So no, the Thanksgiving Pipette didn't make the list.

IZERS

INGREDIENTS

- 8 Scallops, in their shell
- Big Swede BBQ Badass Seafood Boost
- 4 slices Bacon or Pancetta
- 1 cup Sweet Peppers, finely chopped
- Chives, finely chopped for garnish
- Broccoli Sprouts, for garnish
- 2 lbs Kosher Salt

Sea Urchin Sauce:
- 5 Tbs Butter
- 1 Shallot, finely chopped
- 1/2 Tbs Garlic, minced
- 1 1/2 cup Dry White Wine
- 1 cup Seafood Stock
- 6 Sea Urchin Tongues
- 1/2 cup Heavy Cream
- Black Pepper to taste

 **650°F, 343°C
4 MINS**

Grilled Scallops and
SEA URCHIN

SERVES
4–8

TIME
30 MINS

METHOD
GRILLING

This beautiful appetizer tastes like the salty sea with a hint of smoke - it is simply stunning.

METHOD

1. Start by cleaning the scallops so you only have the white meat and the shell. Season the scallops with the Big Swede BBQ Badass Seafood Boost or your favorite Seafood rub.

2. Set your grill to 650°F or 343°C. If using wood or pellets, use pecan wood.

3. Place a cast iron pan on the grill and melt 2 Tbs of butter. Add the shallot and the garlic, and sauté for 2 minutes. Then add rest of the ingredients for the sea urchin sauce and cook for a couple of minutes. Season with black pepper. Remove the pan from the grill and blend the sauce using a blender or mixer until smooth. Set aside.

4. Place the bacon slices on the grill and grill until crispy. When crispy, remove from the grill and let cool. Then break them into small bacon bits.

5. Thread the scallops onto a metal skewer and oil the grates. Grill the scallops for 4 minutes until cooked through or until inner temperature reaches 115°F or 46°C.. Remove the skewer from the grill.

6. Pour all the salt into a serving tray and place the scallop shells on the salt. It will keep the shells steady when plating and serving.

7. Place some bacon bits on the bottom of scallop shells. Then place one scallop on top of the bacon in each shell. Carefully pour the sea urchin sauce around the scallops.

8. Place some of the finely chopped sweet peppers on the scallops. Use multicolored ones for a more beautiful presentation.

9. Garnish with chives and broccoli sprouts and them serve immediately.

INGREDIENTS

- 1 Sourdough Bread, cut in thick slices
- 1 Shallot, finely diced
- 2 lbs Chanterelle Mushrooms, cleaned
- 2 Tbs Butter
- 2 tsp Sea Salt
- 1 Tbs Cognac
- 1/2 cup Heavy Cream
- 1 Tbs Soy Sauce
- 5 slices Bacon
- Chives, finely chopped
- Salt and Pepper

Grilled Chanterelle and Bacon
TOAST

SERVES	TIME	METHOD
4–6	20 MINS	GRILLING

During the fall Swedes love to go out foraging the "Forest Gold" – freshly picked chanterelle mushrooms. This toast is my favorite way to eat these golden nuggets.

METHOD

1. Set up your grill for two-zone grilling with one hot side and one colder side.

2. Place a heavy cast iron pan over the hot zone of the grill.

3. Cook the bacon slices in the pan until crispy and then remove, 4–5 minutes. Let them rest. When cold, break them into small bacon bits. Remove the bacon fat from the pan and set aside for later use.

4. Melt 1 Tbs of butter in the pan and then add the finely diced shallot. Sauté for 1 minute then add the mushrooms and the sea salt.

5. Cook the mushrooms over high heat until they have released all the liquid, about 6–8 minutes. When they start making a snapping sound, add the rest of the butter and brown the mushrooms for two more minutes.

6. Move the cast iron pan over to the colder side of the grill

and deglaze the pan with the cognac. Reduce for 1 minute.

7. Add the heavy cream and the soy sauce and simmer over lower heat until reduced by half. Stir constantly because the cream can break if it gets too hot. Season with salt and pepper to taste.

9. While the mushroom stew is finishing, slice the sourdough bread into thick slices. Brush each side with the bacon fat. Grill both sides of the sourdough bread slices for 30 seconds each over the hot side of the grill, or until they have nice grillmarks and getting a slight char. Remove from the grill and let cool for 1 minute.

10. Place a large dollop of chanterelles on top of the bread slices. Then sprinkle the chanterelles with bacon and finally top the toasts with the chopped chives. Serve immediately.

Black Garlic BBQ Sauce with
SMOKED SUNCHOKES

SERVES	TIME	METHOD
3-4	45 MINS	SMOKING

INGREDIENTS

- 1 lb Sunchokes
- Dill
- Extra Virgin Olive Oil
- 8 cloves Black Garlic
- 2 Tbs Black Bean Garlic Sauce
- 1/2 tsp Five Spice powder
- 1/2 cup of Shao Xing Rice Wine
- 1/4 cup Hoisin Sauce
- 3 Tbs Agave Honey
- 2/3 cup Soy sauce
- 1/2 cup White Sugar

**350°F, 177°C
45 MINS**

METHOD

1. Peel and finely mince the black garlic. Put garlic, rice wine, hoisin sauce, honey, sugar, bean sauce, and five spice in a blender and purée.

2. Simmer the mixture in a large saucepan over medium heat for 10 minutes until it bubbles, and the sauce begins to thicken. Set aside while preparing the sunchokes.

3. Set the smoker to 350°F or 177°C. If using wood or pellets, use fruit wood.

4. Scrub the sunchokes thoroughly. Make sure to rinse of all the dirt. When clean, cut the sunchokes in half.

5. Pour 3 Tbs of olive oil into an oven-proof pan.

6. Place sunchokes cut-side down in the pan and insert into smoker. Smoke the sunchokes for 20 minutes until they have softened slightly and browned. Turn and smoke for another 15 minutes.

7. After about 35 minutes, remove pan from smoker. Dip the sunchokes into the BBQ sauce and make sure that they are covered in sauce. Place them in the pan again and smoke for 5 minutes. Repeat this procedure one more time.

8. Cut the thick stalks from the dill and chop. Sprinkle dill over sunchokes. Serve immediately.

Marinated and Grilled
CREMINIS

SERVES	TIME	METHOD
2-4	10 MINS	GRILLING

METHOD

1. Rinse and clean the cremini mushrooms and remove all dirt. Also remove the stalks.

2. Swirl half the butter in a small saucepan over medium heat until melted. Add the garlic and soften about 2 minutes. Stir in the soy sauce.

3. Put the mushrooms in a medium bowl, add the soy-garlic butter and toss until well coated. Marinate for 30-60 minutes.

4. Thread the mushrooms on the skewers, putting 7 to 8 on each and leaving 3-inch handles at the ends. If using wooden skewers, soak the wooden skewers in water first for 20 minutes.

5. Melt the rest of the butter and mix with the Big Swede BBQ Badass Veggie Boost or your favorite herb seasoning. Set aside and use for basting.

6. Set up your grill for direct grilling and high heat, 650°F or 343°C.

7. Grill the mushrooms, turning the skewers every 2 minutes. Brush with the butter-veggie boost mix after every turn, until the mushrooms are slightly charred all over and softened, 8 to 9 minutes. Remove from skewers and serve immediately.

INGREDIENTS

- 1 1/2 lb Cremini Mushrooms
- 6 Tbs Butter, unsalted
- 3 cloves Garlic, minced
- 1 1/2 Tbs Soy Sauce
- 2 Tbs Big Swede BBQ Badass Veggie Boost

**650°F, 343°C
10 MINS**

Smoked Buffalo
CHICKEN DIP

SERVES
4-6

TIME
60 MINS

METHOD
SMOKING

Smoked Buffalo Chicken Dip might just be the best party dish ever invented

INGREDIENTS

- **2 lbs Chicken Thighs, boneless and skinless**
- **Big Swede BBQ Badass Bird Boost**
- **3 cups Chicken Broth**
- **16 oz Cream Cheese**
- **1 cup Hot Sauce**
- **1 cup Buttermilk Ranch Dressing**
- **1 cup Shredded Cheese Blend**
- **1 cup Blue Cheese Crumbles**
- **Chives, finely chopped for topping**

METHOD

1. Trim some of the extra fat and silverskin from the boneless and skinless chicken thighs.

2. Season the chicken thighs generously with the Big Swede BBQ Badass Bird Boost or your favorite poultry seasoning.

3. Set your grill or smoker to 225°F or 107°C. If using wood or pellets, use fruit wood.

4. Smoke the chicken thighs for 30 minutes and then remove from grill.

5. Place the smoked chicken thighs in a crockpot and cover with the stock. Cook on slow overnight.

6. Remove chicken thighs from the crockpot and shred in a bowl. Add a few scoops of the braising liquid to add some more moisture into the shredded chicken.

7. Add the cream cheese, hot sauce, buttermilk ranch dressing and shredded cheese blend to the chicken and mix carefully.

8. Scoop the buffalo chicken dip into an ovenproof pan.

9. Crumble the blue cheese on top of the buffalo chicken dip.

10. Set the temperature on your grill or smoker to 350°F or 177°C.

11. Insert the buffalo chicken dip and smoke for 30 minutes or until the dip and the blue cheese crumbles are starting to melt.

12. Remove from the grill and top with finely chopped chives.

13. Serve immediately with your favorite tortilla chips.

Pizzaroni
POPPERS

SERVES **TIME** **METHOD**
4–6 **4 MINS** **GRILLING**

Great party poppers that taste just like Pepperoni Pizza

METHOD

1. Cut the Anaheim peppers in half and remove both the seeds and the inner walls to form a boatlike shape.

2. Brush the inside of the Anaheim peppers with plenty of the authentic pizza sauce.

3. Season the inside of the peppers with our Big Swede BBQ Badass Veggie Boost or your favorite herb seasoning.

4. Mix the cream cheese and the mozzarella in a bowl and make sure that it is thoroughly blended.

5. Quarter the pepperoni slices and then chop them into small chunks.

6. Fill each pepper with the cheese mix making sure you fill in the whole pepper. Then sprinkle each pepper with plenty of the pepperoni chunks.

7. Light or set your grill to direct hot heat, about 650°F or 345°C. If using wood or charcoal, use fruit wood like cherry, peach or apple.

8. Carefully place the peppers on the hot grill grates and grill over direct heat until they have a good char and the cheese is starting to melt. Don't cook them too long, the peppers need to have a little structure left and a nice chew. Mushy peppers will only fall apart when serving them.

9. Torch the top side with a blow torch to char the pepperoni chunks and give the cheese a nice golden color.

10. Remove from the grill and let rest for a couple of minutes before serving. This will allow the peppers to cool down a little and be easier to handle when eating.

- 4 Anaheim Peppers
- 1/2 cup Authentic Pizza Sauce (see Pizza chapter)
- Big Swede BBQ Badass Veggie Boost
- 8 oz Cream Cheese, Chive and Onion flavored
- 8 oz Mozzarella Cheese, shredded
- 4 oz Pepperonis, finely sliced

650°F, 343°C
4 MINS

Smoked Duck Breast
CROSTINI

SERVES	TIME	METHOD
4-6	50 MINS	SMOKING

INGREDIENTS

- 1 Moulard Duck Breast
- Big Swede BBQ Badass Texas Boost
- 3 Tbs Fresh Horseradish, grated
- 1 cup Creme Fraiche
- 1/2 Tbs Garlic, minced
- 1 tsp Salt
- 1 Sourdough Baguette, sliced into 1-inch slices
- Old Fashioned Mustard
- 1 cup Sweet Peppers, finely chopped
- Broccoli Sprouts, for garnish

METHOD

1. Score the duckbreast in a tight criss-cross pattern. Be careful not to penetrate the meat. Season the duckbreast on both sides with the Big Swede BBQ Badass Texas Boost or your favorite SPG rub. Place the duckbreast fat side up on a baker rack in an aluminum pan.

2. Set your smoker or grill to 225°F or 107°C. If using wood or pellets, use pecan wood.

3. Insert the aluminum pan with the duckbreast in the smoker. Smoke for 45 minutes or until the duck breast reaches an inner temperature of 120°F or 49°C.

4. While the duck breast is smoking, prepare the horseradish creme. Mix the creme fraiche and the freshly grated horseradish in a bowl. Start with adding 2/3 of the horseradish, taste and then add more if needed. Add the garlic and season with the salt.

4. When ready, remove the pan with the duckbreast from the smoker and increase the temperature of the smoker or grill to 550°F or 288°C.

6. Place the duckbreast fat side down and sear it for a couple of minutes. Also brush the baguette slices with the duckfat from the pan and grill for 2 minutes as well. Remove the bread when nicely charred.

7. When the duckbreast reaches an inner temperature of 135°F or 57°C, remove from the grill and let it rest for 5 minutes. Then slice into thin slices against the grain.

8. Spread a thin layer of the mustard on each baguette slice. Then place one or two slices of duck breast on top. Add a dollop of the horseradish cream and top with the sweet peppers. Garnish with the broccoli sprouts and serve immediately.

Grilled Jalapeno
POPPERS

SERVES 4-6   **TIME** 15 MINS   **METHOD** BAKING

INGREDIENTS

- 18 whole Jalapenos
- 18 strips Bacon
- 10 oz Cream Cheese
- 1 1/2 cup Cheddar Cheese
- Big Swede BBQ Badass Pork Boost

METHOD

1. Set your grill or smoker to 400°F or 204°C. If using wood or pellets, use pecan or maple wood.

2. Wash the jalapenos. Remove the stem and cut them into halves. Deseed the core and remove the membranes.

3. Place the cream cheese in a microwave safe bowl and heat in the microwave for 30 seconds. Combine softened cream cheese, cheddar cheese, and 1 Tbs of the Big Swede BBQ Badass Pork Boost or your favorite sweet BBQ rub into a mixing bowl. Mix the ingredients until well combined.

4. Fill the jalapenos with the cream cheese and cheddar mix.

5. Cut each bacon slice in half and wrap 1/2 slice of bacon around each filled pepper. Secure the bacon with toothpick

6. Season the poppers with the Big Swede BBQ Badass Pork Boost or your favorite sweet bbq rub.

7. Place the poppers in the smoker or grill and bake for 15 minutes or until bacon is fully cooked. and browned and the cheese is melting.

8. Remove the poppers from the grill and let cool for 3 minutes. Remove the toothpicks and serve immediately.

- 20 Baked Donutholes
- 1 package Bacon
- Big Swede BBQ Badass Pork Boost
- Artisanal Pure Maple Syrup

Bacon Wrapped
DONUT HOLES

SERVES	TIME	METHOD
4-6	15 MINS	GRILLING

METHOD

1. Set your grill or smoker to 400°F or 204°C. If using wood or pellets, use peach or apple.

2. Cut the bacon slices in half lengthwise. Wrap each baked donuthole with the bacon. Secure with a toothpick.

3. When all the donutholes are baconwrapped – sprinkle generously with the Big Swede BBQ Badass Pork Boost or your favorite sweet BBQ rub.

4. Place on a baker's rack in the smoker until the bacon is getting crispy, 10–15 minutes. Flip the donutholes occasionally.

5. When ready, remove from the grill and drizzle with maple syrup. Serve immediately.

 400°F or 204°C.
15 MINS

This recipe is inspired by my friend Dominic Gonzales who makes the best roasted tomatillo salsa I have ever tried. This is not his exact recipe but it is close. Darn close. And it is also darn tasty.

INGREDIENTS

- 10 Tomatillos
- 1 Yellow Onion
- 2 Fresno Peppers
- 12 Jalapenos
- 2 Caribe Peppers
- 2 Whole Garlic Bulbs
- 5 Roma Tomatoes
- 2 Tbs Big Swede BBQ Badass Burger Boost
- 1 bunch Cilantro, chopped
- 1 Tbs Cumin
- 3 cups Chicken Broth
- 1/2 Can Chipotle Peppers in Adobo Sauce

Roasted Tomatillo
SALSA

SERVES	TIME	METHOD
4-6	20 MINS	GRILLING

METHOD

1. Set up your grill or smoker for direct grilling high heat, 650°F or 343°C. If using wood or pellets, use oak wood. If possible, set it up so you have one hot zone and one warm zone.

2. Roast all the vegetables over the hot zone. When the vegetables have a good char and are cooked through, move them to the warm side of the grill. Some of the vegetables will cook faster than others. Continue until all the vegetables have a good char and are cooked through.

3. Let the roasted vegetables cool for a couple of minutes. Then peel the garlic bulbs and remove some of the charred skin from the peppers.

4. Place all the roasted vegetables in a large stock pot together with the cumin, chipotle peppers in adobo sauce, cilantro and chicken broth.

4. Season the pot with the Big Swede BBQ Badass Burger Boost, or your favorite umami seasoning.

5. Mix with an immersion blender until smooth. Add salt or pepper if needed. Serve with Tortilla Chips.

Grilled Avocado
TOASTS

SERVES	TIME	METHOD
4-6	10 MINS	GRILLING

Grilled guacamole adds a wonderful smoky flavor to these amazing Avocado Toasts

METHOD

1. Set up your grill for direct grilling high heat, 650°F or 343°C.

2. Place the avocados and jalapenos on the grill cut-side down. Also place the onion slices on the grill. Grill until the avocados, jalapenos, and onions start to char, 3 to 5 minutes.

3. Remove from the grill. Finely chop the onion and the jalapeno. Place in a molcajete and mash together with some salt and pepper. When the oils are released, scoop the flesh from the avocados and add to the molcajete as well. Mash the avocados carefully, then add the tomato, the lime juice and the cilantro. Stir and set aside.

4. Spray both sides of the artisan sourdough bread slices with the duckfat spray or brush with extra virgin olive oil.

6. Grill the bread slices on both side until they have nice grillmarks and starting to get a good char. Remove from the grill.

7. Place a large dollop of the grilled guacamole on each toast and season with the Big Swede BBQ Badass Veggie Boost or your favorite herb seasoning.

8. Crumble feta cheese on top of the grilled guacamole (you can also use cotija, parmesan or even blue cheese).

9. Top the grilled avocado toasts with pork rinds (preferably the herb flavored kind) and serve immediately.

INGREDIENTS

- 2 Avocados, ripe and halved
- 1 Roma Tomatoes, chopped with seeds removed
- Red Onion, thinly sliced
- 1 Jalapeno. deseeded and halved
- 2 Tbs Cilantro, finely chopped
- 1/2 Lime, juiced
- Salt and pepper to taste
- Big Swede BBQ Badass Veggie Boost
- Feta Cheese, crumbled
- Pork Rinds, Herbed
- Artisan Sourdough Bread, sliced
- Duckfat Spray

Lingonberry and Jalapeno
BRIE CHEESE

SERVES
3-4

TIME
10 MINS

METHOD
SMOKING

INGREDIENTS

- 2 Brie Cheeses
- 6 Tbs Lingonberry Jam
- 2 Jalapenos
- Big Swede BBQ Badass Veggie Boost

- 1 Cedar plank (preferably a square plank 6 inches square)

400°F, 204°C
10 MINS

METHOD

1. Set up your grill or smoker for direct grilling, 400°F or 204°C. If using wood or pellets, use apple wood.

2. Place the plank directly on the grill grate and grill until dark on one side. Set aside and let cool.

3. Start by stemming and thinly slice the jalapenos crosswise. Place the brie cheeses in the center of the plank. Season lightly on top with the Big Swede BBQ Badass Veggie Boost or your favorite herb seasoning.

4. Spread the lingonberry jam on top of the brie cheeses, using the back of a spoon. Place the jalapenos on top of the jam so the slices overlap in a decorative pattern.

5. Place the plank on the grill. Grill or smoke until the top of the brie cheese browns and the sides are soft and beginning to melt, 8 to 10 minutes.

6. Serve the Brie on the plank hot off the grill. Spread it on grilled bread slices or crackers.

Spinach Filled
PORTABELLAS

SERVES	TIME	METHOD
2-4	15 MINS	GRILLING

INGREDIENTS

- 1 lb Cremini Mushrooms
- 2 Tbs Butter
- 1 Tbs Garlic, minced
- 2 cups Baby Spinach
- 4 Tbs Sour Cream
- 6 Portabella Mushrooms, destemmed
- 1 cup Parmesan cheese, grated
- 1 cup Mozzarella cheese, grated
- Big Swede BBQ Badass Veggie Boost

450°F, 232°C
15 MINS

METHOD

1. Set up your smoker or grill to 450°F or 232°C. If using wood or pellets, use oak wood.

2. Place a heavy cast iron skillet in the grill. When the skillet is hot, add and melt the butter.

3. Clean, destem and quarter the cremini mushrooms. Add the mushrooms and garlic to the pan and sauté in the pan until browned and cooked through, about 4 minutes.

4. After 4 minutes, add the baby spinach to the skillet and cook for another 2 minutes, while stirring.
5. Add the sour cream and stir gently. Remove the mixture from the skillet and set aside.

6. Place the destemmed portabella mushrooms in the skillet. and fill with the sourcream/spinach mixture.

7. Cover with both parmesan and mozzarella cheese and season with the Big Swede BBQ Badass Veggie Boost or your favorite herb seasoning.

8. Grill the mushrooms in the grill for another 5 minutes or until the cheese is melted and golden brown, Remove and serve immediately.

INGREDIENTS

- 1 lb Pork Chorizo
- 10 oz Rotel Original
- 10 oz Rotel Chipotle
- 16 oz Smoked Gouda Cheese, cubed
- 2 lbs Velveeta Cheese, cubed
- 10 oz Cream of Mushroom Soup
- 2 Tbs Big Swede BBQ Badass Beef Boost
- 1 Tbs Chipotles in Adobo Sauce
- 3/4 cup Cilantro, chopped

Smoked
QUESO DIP

SERVES
4–6

TIME
60 MINS

METHOD
SMOKING

This smoked queso dip is the perfect appetizer to share with your guests and the flavor possibilities are endless. I add chipotle peppers both for heat and a deep smoky flavor.

METHOD

1. Set up your smoker or grill to 350°F or 177°C. If using wood or pellets, use oak wood.

2. Heat up a big cast iron pan in the smoker and when hot, add the chorizo. Brown for about 10 minutes. Remove the cast iron from the smoker and drain any excess chorizo fat.

3. Add the 2 cans of Rotel to the pan. Substitute any of the cans with your own personal favorite to make your own flavor profile.

4. Add the cubed gouda and velveeta cheese to the pan. Also add cream of mushroom soup. Season with the Big Swede BBQ Badass Beef Boost or your favorite BBQ

rub. Last, add a spoonful of sauce from a can of Chipotle peppers in adobo sauce. This will give a great heat but also a wonderful smoky flavor to the queso.

5. Place the cast iron pan, uncovered, in your smoker for 45 minutes. Stir thoroughly every 10 minutes to ensure that the queso doesn't burn.

6. Finely chop the cilantro and add to the pan as well. Cook for another 5–10 minutes

7. When ready, remove from smoker and serve immediately with tortilla chips. You can also garnish the queso with diced tomatoes and some cilantro.

Grilled Cheese
SANDWICH

SERVES	TIME	METHOD
4-8	10 MINS	GRILLING

Cheese, cheese, and even more cheese - sometimes more is better

INGREDIENTS

- 8 slices Sourdough Bread
- 6 Tbs Butter
- 4 Tbs Mayonnaise
- 4 Tbs Parmesan Cheese
- 8 slices Sharp White Cheddar Cheese
- 8 slices Monterey Jack Cheese
- 8 slices Gruyere Cheese
- 4 oz Brie Cheese, rind removed and sliced
- Big Swede BBQ Badass Veggie Boost

METHOD

1. Set your smoker or grill to 550°F or 288°C. If using wood or pellets, use apple or cherry wood.

2. Spread half of the butter on one side of the bread slices. Place the bread butter-side down on the grill and grill until golden brown, 2-3 minutes. When ready, remove from the grill and set aside.

3. In a small bowl, mix mayonnaise, parmesan cheese, and the remaining butter.

4. To assemble the sandwiches, top toasted side of 4 bread slices with the sliced Brie, Cheddar, Monterey and Gruyere cheese. Season with the Big Swede BBQ Badass Veggie Boost or your favorite herb seasoning,

5. Place the remaining bread slices on top of the cheese slices with the toasted side facing inward. Spread mayonnaise mixture on the outsides of each sandwich. Place on the grill and cook until bread is golden brown and cheese is melted, 2-3 minutes on each side. Remove the bread from the grill. Slice diagonally and serve immediately.

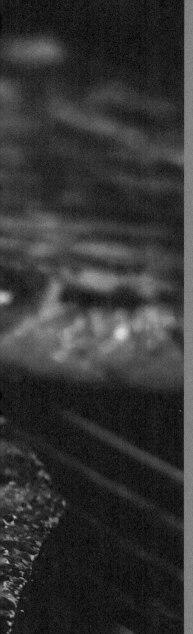

Beef

Who doesn't love a great steak?
In many ways, beef is the king of meat. It is flavorful, there are many ways to cook it, because there are so many different cuts, and they are all really, really good!!

I love cooking beef. The aromas in the backyard when you throw a well-seasoned steak on the hot grillgrates always bring a big smile to my face. Or those wonderful moments in life when the smoke slowly rises to the sky in the early morning mist from the smoker, and you can smell hints of the brisket cooking inside and slowly turning into melt-in-your mouth meat candy.

I find that people also struggle with beef. I have tasted plenty of overcooked steaks at barbeques. I have had my fair share of tough and rubbery brisket slices at BBQ restaurants. There are some basic rules that applies to all backyard cooking but perhaps even more so when it comes to cooking beef: Always season the beef well in advance, Cook to temperature and doneness, rather than time. And always let the beef rest to allow the juices to evenly distribute back into the meat after cooking.

And a steak should be served medium-rare.

BEEF

INGREDIENTS

- 2 Ribeye Steaks
- 1 Big Swede BBQ Badass Texas Boost
- Big Swede BBQ Badass Beef Boost
- •• Kosher Salt

Finishing butter:
- 1/2 cup Beef Suet
- 1/2 cup Butter, unsalted
- 1/2 cup Bone Marrow
- 1/2 cup Brisket Drippings

Competition Ribeye

STEAKS

SERVES	TIME	METHOD
2-3	8 MINUTES	GRILLING

It might seem like a lot of steps but when you bite into the Best. Steak. Ever. Period. it will be worth it

METHOD

1. Start with cutting the beef suet (the fat around the beef kidney) and the beef bone marrow into small chunks. Render the suet and the marrow under very low heat for 45 minutes. When the beef suet pieces are browning, pour the rendered fat through a sieve. Mix butter and brisket drippings with the fat and set aside. Keep hot and heat up further just before using.

2. Prepare the grill for direct heat together with grillgrates. Aim for a grate temperature of 630°F or 332°C.

3. Remove excess fat from each ribeye along with any silver skin.

4. Salt brine the steak by covering it in kosher salt for about 30 minutes – dip the steak in a water bath to rinse the steak and remove all the salt.

5. Use an onion holder to poke the steak all around, especially in the fatty parts. Loosely shape the steak and use butcher twine to hold it together. You can also secure the steak using toothpicks to keep it together during grilling.

6. Season each side of the steak with the Big Swede BBQ Badass Texas Boost and rest in a cooler for 30 minutes, then add a layer of the Big Swede BBQ Badass Beef Boost.

7. Place each ribeye on grill grate and set timer for 2 minutes. Place a steak press on top to provide light pressure on the steak. Twist each ribeye 90° and move to a hot part of the grillgrates and grill additional 2 minutes. Clean the spot where the steak was sitting on the grillgrates during each turn. It will keep the searmarks precise and make the steak look perfect.

8. Turn ribeyes over and cook for 1 minute 45 seconds. Baste with finishing butter, turn each steak 90°, and remove from grill when internal temperature reaches 128°F or 53°C on instant read thermometer. Total cook time is approximately 8 minutes.

9. Rest ribeyes for 5-7 minutes with some finishing butter before serving.

Smoked Beans and
BEEF RIBS

SERVES	TIME	METHOD
6–8	10 HRS	SMOKING

METHOD

1. Set your smoker or grill to 250°F or 121°C. If using wood or pellets, use mesquite or oak wood.

2. If your beef ribs have the fat cap still attached, use a sharp filet knife to trim slightly. Leave the membrane on the bones on. Pat dry with paper towel.

3. Mix the salt, pepper and Big Swede BBQ Badass Beef Boost or your favorite beef rub in a bowl. Season the beef ribs generously all over.

4. Place the beef ribs in the smoker. Combine the water and vinegar in a spray bottle. Once the rack has been smoking for at least 2 hours, spritz with the vinegar mixture every hour or so. When the beef ribs reaches an inner temperature of 170°F or 77°C, wrap in butcher paper and place it back in smoker. Smoke until the beef ribs

reach an internal temperature of 204°F or 96°C.

5. Remove the ribs from the smoker. Let them rest in a cooler for at least an hour.

6. While the beef ribs are resting, increase the temperature in the smoker to 375°F or 190°F.

7. Heat butter in a large cast iron pan and sauté the onion and garlic in hot oil until the onion begins to soften. Add bacon and jalapenos, and then cook and stir until bacon is browned. Add beer, BBQ sauce, brown sugar, and molasses into the skillet and stir. Also add the pinto beans and stir. Season with salt and black pepper. Cook in the grill until bubbling and browned, about 45 minutes.

8. Slice the beef ribs between bone and serve together with the smoked beans.

INGREDIENTS

- 8 lb Beef ribs
- 1/2 cup Coarse Sea Salt
- 1/2 cup Black Tellicherri Pepper
- 1/2 cup Big Swede BBQ Badass Beef Boost
- 1/4 cup Vinegar
- 3/4 cup Water

Smoked Beans
- 1 Tbs Butter
- 1 Red Onion, diced
- 3 cloves Garlic, minced
- 1 lb Peppered Bacon, diced
- 3 Jalapenos, minced
- 1 cup Guinness Beer
- 1 cup BBQ Sauce
- 1/2 cup Brown Sugar
- 2 Tbs Molasses
- 6 cups cooked Pinto Beans
- Salt and pepper to taste

250°F, 121°C
10 HRS

INGREDIENTS

- 1 Tomahawk Steak
- Big Swede BBQ Badass Texas Boost
- Big Swede BBQ Badass Beef Boost
- 1 stick Butter, unsalted

Few thing tastes better than when you first smoke a great steak and then sear it for maximum flavor.

Reverse Seared Tomahawk
STEAK

METHOD

1. Place the steak on a large cutting board and let it come to room temperature. Season first lightly with the Big Swede BBQ Badass Texas Boost or your favorite SPG rub on both sides. Then season lightly on both sides with the Big Swede BBQ Badass Beef Boost or your favorite beef rub. Let it rest for 45 minutes while starting up the grill.

2. Set up your grill for indirect grilling so you have one hot zone and one colder zone. If using wood or charcoal, use oak wood.

3. Place the tomahawk steak in the indirect zone of the grill. Grill steak for 30 minutes on indirect heat until it reaches internal temperature of 125°F or 50°C.

4. Once ready, move the tomahawk steak to be directly over the heat. Flip every 20 seconds for 3-4 minutes, or until the outer layer develops a desired amount of crust on the outside. Remove the tomahawk steak when it has an internal temperature of 135°F or 57°C.

5. Place a couple of slices of butter on top of the steak. Leave to rest for 10 minutes before slicing.

INGREDIENTS

- 2 lbs Ground Chuck
- 1/2 lb Ground Brisket
- 1/2 lb Ground Short Rib
- 3 Tbs Big Swede BBQ Badass Burger Boost
- 4 Brioche Buns
- 2 Tbs Butter
- 1 1/2 cup Crispy Onions
- American Cheese
- Duckfat spray

Garlic Aioli:
- 2 Egg Yolks
- 2 Garlic Cloves, finely minced
- 1 tsp Dijon Mustard
- 2 Tbs Lemon Juice
- 1 tsp Kosher Salt
- 1/2 cup Vegetable Oil
- 1/2 cup Extra Virgin Olive Oil

Grilled
SMASH BURGERS

SERVES
3-4

TIME
5 MINS

METHOD
GRIDDLE GRILLING

"Smashing" burgers creates more surface area for the Maillard reaction to take place – and it is in that thin caramelized crust all the flavor is.

METHOD

1. Using a large whisk, combine the egg yolks, garlic, Dijon mustard, lemon juice, and salt in a medium bowl. Whisk constantly and add a few drops of vegetable oil to the egg mixture. Continue adding drops and whisking until the mixture starts to thicken. When well combined, add the vegetable oil in a thin stream, always whisking. Continue with the olive oil. Set aside in the fridge.

2. Mix the ground meat with the Big Swede BBQ Badass Burger Boost or your favorite umami seasoning. Loosely roll and pack the ground meat mix into small balls, about 2-3 ounces for each burger.

3. Set your griddle to really hot or place a large cast iron pan on a hot grill, about 650°F or 343°C.

4. Place the balls on the griddle and smash with a firm spatula or burger press to your desired thinness. Flip the burger after about 90 seconds and sprinkle with additional Big Swede BBQ Badass Burger Boost.

5. Add a slice of American cheese to each burger patty.

6. While grilling the burgers, melt the butter on the griddle and toast the cut side of the burger buns in the butter until golden brown. Remove when ready.

7. Spread a healthy amount of garlic aioli on the bottom bun, then place 2-3 patties with cheese on top. Sprinkle some crispy onions on the patties and then place the top bun on top. Serve immediately.

47

METHOD

1. Preheat your smoker or grill to 275°F or 135°C. If using wood or pellets, use oak wood.

2. Season the pork belly slices with the Big Swede BBQ Badass Pork Boost or your favorite sweet BBQ rub. Place the pork belly slices in the grill and smoke until they reach an inner temperature of 165°F or 74°C.

3. Carefully score the beef franks in a criss-cross pattern using a sharp knife. This will help the BBQ rub to stick better, but also infuse the beef franks with more smoke flavor. Season the beef franks with the BBQ seasoning as well.

4. Add the beef franks to the smoker as well and smoke until the pork belly slices hits an inner temperature of 200°F or 93°F and the beef franks are cooked through.

5. While the beef franks and pork belly slices are smoking, prepare the Pico de Gallo and Cilantro Lime Crema. To make the Pico de Gallo, dice the tomatoes, onion, jalapeno, cilantro, and garlic and toss together. Add lime and salt and pepper.

6. Place all the ingredients for the Cilantro Lime Crema in a food processor and combine well. Pour into a squeeze bottle and set aside.

7. When the pork belly slices and beef franks are ready, remove from the smoker and start building the Sonoran dog.

8. Place a slice of pork belly together with a smoked beef frank in a bun. Spread some hatch chile guacamole on one side of the bun and some salsa on the other. Slather the Sonoran dog with the pico de gallo. Add grilled onions on top and then crumble some cotija cheese over the onions. Drizzle the Sonoran dogs with the Cilantro Lime Crema. Finally, top it off with some cilantro leaves. Serve immediately.

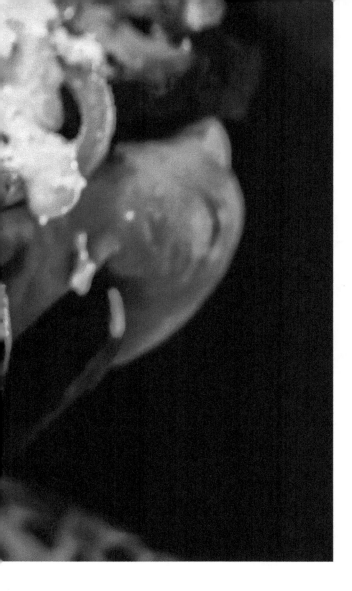

INGREDIENTS

- Quarter Pound Beef Franks
- Large Hot Dog Buns
- Crumbled Cotija Cheese
- Roasted Garlic and Tomatillo Salsa
- Hatch Chile Guacamole
- Cilantro
- Big Swede BBQ Badass Pork Boost
- 1 lb Pork Belly, thinly sliced
- Salt and pepper, to taste
- Grilled Onions

Fresh Pico De Gallo:
- 3 Garlic Cloves
- 1 Jalapeno
- 1/2 Lime
- 1/2 Red Onion
- 5 Roma Tomatoes
- 1/2 bunch Cilantro
- Salt and Pepper

Cilantro Lime Crema:
- 3/4 cup Sour cream
- 1/4 cup Mayonnaise
- 1/4 cup fresh Cilantro leaves
- Juice and zest of a lime
- Sea salt, to taste

Smoked

SONORAN DOG

SERVES	TIME	METHOD
4–6	60 MINS	SMOKING

Here in the Arizona, our local delicacy is the Sonoran dog. This pork belly wrapped hot dog is loaded with southwestern flavors and is the perfect dish when we have out-of-state guests.

Chimichurri and
PICANHA

SERVES
4–6

TIME
10 MINS

METHOD
GRILLING

50

INGREDIENTS

- 3 lbs Picanha
- Flaky Sea Salt

- Chimichurri Sauce:
- 1 cup Italian Parsley, chopped
- 1 cup Cilantro, chopped
- 1 Shallot, chopped
- 7 cloves Garlic chopped
- 4 tsp Big Swede, BBQ Badass Texas Boost
- 1 cup Olive Oil
- 2 Tbs White Wine Vinegar
- 3 Tbs Lime Juice

**650°F, 345°C
10 MINS**

METHOD

1. Set up your grill for direct grilling high heat, 650°F or 343°C. If using wood or pellets. use oak or hickory wood.

2. Place the finely chopped cilantro, parsley, garlic and shallot in a bowl. Add the Big Swede BBQ Badass Texas Boost or your favorite SPG rub, the white wine vinegar and the lime juice and mix.

3. Whisking slowly, drizzle in the olive oil and blend until thoroughly mixed. Set aside.

4. Trim excess fat from the picanha and then slice it into individual steaks with the grain.

5. Season both sides heavily with flaky sea salt and then allow the steaks to sweat for at least an hour.

6. When the grill is hot, place the picanha on the grill. Grill for 8-10 minutes and flip the steaks every 2 minutes. Picanha has a thick fat cap so watch out for flare-ups. Move the picanha around on the grill to avoid burning the meat. When the picanha reaches and inner temperature of 135°F or 57°C, remove the steaks from the grill

7. Let the steaks rest for 5 minutes then slice against the grain. Serve immediately with the chimichurri sauce.

Picanha is the highlight at any churrasco (Brazilian barbecue). If you haven't had it before, you're going to want to try it at your next BBQ

METHOD

1. Start my mixing together the ground beef, pork, and veal in a large mixing bowl. In another mixing bowl, mix the breadcrumbs, the cream and the whole milk. When mixed and soaked, pour the breadcrumb mix into the ground meat and mix by hand.

2. Add the sautéed onion, soy sauce, Dijon mustard, eggs and the Big Swede BBQ Badass Burger Boost or your favorite umami rub to the mix. Mix thoroughly by hand.

3. Dip your hands in cold water and then roll and shape the meatballs. Place the meatballs on a baking rack.

4. Place lingonberries in a bowl. Add the sugar and stir every 15 minutes or so for about an hour. When the sugar is completely dissolved, set aside.

5. Set your smoker or grill to 235°F or 113°C. Use oak or hickory wood for a good flavor and color.

6. Place the meatballs in the smoker or grill and smoke for 45 minutes. Remove from the grill.

7. Increase the temperature in the grill to 500°F or 260°C. Insert at large cast iron skillet into the grill and heat up. When hot, add the olive oil and the butter.

8. Add the meatballs to the hot pan and brown them on all the sides for about 7-8 minutes. Remove the meatballs from the pan.

9. Add some more butter in the pan. When melted add the Dijon mustard, heavy cream, beef broth, flour and red currant jelly and whisk until the flour is completely dissolved. Season with salt and pepper to taste.

10. Pour all meatballs into the cream sauce and let simmer for 3-4 minutes. When ready, remove the pan from the grill

11. Serve the smoked Swedish meatballs with the cream sauce, lingonberries and some boiled or roasted potatoes.

INGREDIENTS

- 1 lb Ground Beef, 75/25
- 1/2 lb Ground Pork
- 1/2 lb Ground Veal
- 1 cup Breadcrumbs
- 1/2 cup Heavy Cream
- 1/2 cup Whole Milk
- 1 1/2 Onion, chopped and browned
- 2 Eggs
- 1 Tbs Soy Sauce
- 1 Tbs Dijon Mustard
- 2 Tbs Big Swede BBQ Badass Burger Boost
- 1 Tbs Extra Virgin Olive Oil
- 2 Tbs Butter

Cream Sauce:
- 1 Tbs Butter
- 1 Tbs Dijon Mustard
- 3 Tbs Beef Broth, concentrated
- 2 cups Heavy Cream
- 1 Tbs Red Currant Jelly
- 2 Tbs Flour
- Salt and pepper to taste

Lingonberries:
1 cup Wild Lingonberries

- Roasted or Boiled Potatoes

Smoked Swedish

MEATBALLS

SERVES	TIME	METHOD
4-6	1 HR	SMOKING

There are just as many meatball recipes in Sweden as there are Swedes. We all have our favorite way of making these. But I think my mom made the best meatballs ever. They were small and packed with flavors so here is my homage to her version. I added a kiss of smoke to elevate the taste even more.

Smoked Asian
HOT DOGS

SERVES | **TIME** | **METHOD**
4-6 | **75 MINS** | **SMOKING**

There are almost endless ways to "chef up" regular hot dogs but this is one of my favorites - and it is packed with bold asian flavors

METHOD

1. Set up your smoker or grill to 250°F or 121°C. If using wood or pellets, use cherry wood.

2. Score the skin of the beef franks in a criss-cross pattern on two sides. Place the franks in the smoker and smoke for 60 minutes.

3. Mix the ketchup, soy sauce, sriracha powder and ginger powder in a bowl and set aside.

4. Mix the shredded slaw mix and the sesame dressing in another bowl and set aside.

5. Remove the beef franks from the grill and place in an aluminum pan. Pour the gochujang sauce and the BBQ sauce in the pan, and coat the beef franks thoroughly. Make sure that all the beef franks are glazed with the spicy bbq sauce.

6. Increase the temperature in the smoker to 550°F or 288°C. Place the glazed beef franks back in the smoker and grill until the BBQ sauce is set, about 5 minutes. Turn frequently so the sauce doesn't burn. Also spray the inside of the buns with some oil and grill the buns until they have nice grill marks. Remove both buns and franks from the smoker.

7. Start by spreading some of the ketchup mix on the bread. By closing and then opening the bread again, it will spread evenly. Then scatter some of the finely chopped kimchi on the bread and place the beef franks in the buns. Cover the franks with the sesame slaw. Next, sprinkle green onions, toasted sesame seeds and cilantro leaves on top of the slaw and finally drizzle the Asian hot dogs with the sriracha mayonnaise. Serve immediately.

INGREDIENTS

- 6 Large Beef Franks
- 1 cup Ketchup
- 2 Tbs Soy Sauce
- 2 Tbs Sriracha Powder
- 2 cups Shredded Slaw Mix
- 4 Tbs Sesame Dressing
- 1 cup Gochujang Sauce
- 1 cup BBQ Sauce
- 6 Hot Dog Buns
- 1/2 cup Kimchi, finely chopped
- Sriracha Mayonnaise
- Toasted Sesame Seeds, for garnish
- Cilantro Leaves, for garnish
- Green Onions, chopped for garnish

**650°F, 345°C
10 MINS**

INGREDIENTS

- 1 lb Ribeye Steak, sliced extremely thin
- 15 oz Cheez Whiz
- 1 Yellow Onion, diced
- 2 Deli rolls
- 3 tsp Big Swede BBQ Badass Texas Boost
- 2 Tbs Canola Oil

METHOD

1. Light or set your grill or griddle to direct hot heat, about 650°F or 345°C. If using wood or charcoal, use white or red oak.

2. Heat up a small sauce pan over low heat. Pour the cheez wiz into the pan and slowly heat up until pourable. Keep warm until used.

3. Place a large cast iron skillet on the grill and add the canola oil. Heat up the oil for 2 minutes.

4. Add the onions and 1 tsp of the Big Swede BBQ Badass Texas Boost or your favorite SPG rub and cook, stirring frequently, until translucent, about 7 minutes.

5. Add the thinly sliced steak, and season with the Big Swede BBQ Badass Texas Boost, about 2 tsps. Cook for about 3 minutes, turning the beef and the onions occasionally.

6. Divide the cooked beef in the pan into two piles, about the length of each roll. Pour 1/3 of the cheez whiz on top of each and let the cheese melt over the steak.

7. Lay a split roll over each pile of beef, so it looks like an upside-down sandwich. Working one sandwich at a time, slide a long spatula beneath one pile of steak, and flip it right-side up onto a plate. Repeat with the second cheesesteak.

8. Pour the last 1/3 of the cheez whiz on top of the philly cheesesteaks, cut them in half, and serve immediately.

Grilled Philly
CHEESESTEAK

SERVES
2-4

TIME
10 MINS

METHOD
GRILLING

I like my Philly Cheesesteaks "one whiz wit" which equals an Hoagie roll packed with juicy steak, Cheez Whiz and fried onions.

INGREDIENTS

- 1 A5 Wagyu Steak
- Sea Salt, flaky
- 1/4 cup Artisanal Soy Sauce
- 1 Garlic Clove, minced
- 2 Tbs Mirin Rice Wine
- 2 tsp Sesame Oil
- 2 Tbs White Sugar
- 3 Tbs Green Onion, finely sliced
- 1 Tbs Toasted Sesame Seeds
- Flaky Artisanal Sea Salt, for dipping

Yakiniku Sauce and
A5 WAGYU STEAK

SERVES
4–6

TIME
15 MINS

METHOD
GRIDDLE GRILLING

The A5 Wagyu Steak might just be the best steak you will ever have

METHOD

1. Bring the A5 Wagyu stripsteak up to room temperature. Trim off some of the excess fat and shape into a beautiful steak. Save the trimmed fat.

2. Season gently on both sides with coarse sea salt of high quality. Let the steak rest with the salt for at least 35 minutes.

3. Mix the soy sauce, garlic clove, mirin rice wine, sesame oil and white sugar in a small sauce pan and bring to boil over medium heat. Simmer for 3 minutes until all the sugar is dissolved. Then add the green onions and sesame seeds and set aside.

4. Light or set your grill to direct hot heat, about 650°F or 345°C. If using wood or charcoal, use white or red oak.

5. Place a cast iron pan on the grill and make sure it is screaming hot. Melt some of the trimmed fat in the pan. Then place the A5 Wagyu steak in the pan and cook for 2–3 minutes and turn the steak every 20 seconds. Do NOT overcook it.

6. Remove the steak from the pan and rest it for 5 minutes. Then slice into thin slices. Serve immediately.

7. I think the best way to eat A5 Wagyu steak is to dip one end of the steak in either the yakiniku sauce or the flaky sea salt and then just enjoy the complex and rich flavors – it is almost a life changing experience.

Grilled New York Strip with

GORGONZOLA

SERVES	TIME	METHOD
3-4	20 MINS	GRILLING+FRYING

INGREDIENTS

- 2 New York Strip Steaks
- Big Swede BBq Badass Beef Boost
- Flaky Sea Salt to taste

Gorgonzola Sauce:
- 1 cup Heavy Cream
- 1/2 cup Gorgonzola, crumbled
- 1/3 cup Saint Agur Blue, crumbled
- Freshly Ground Pepper to taste
- 2 Tbs Parsley, chopped

French Fries:
- 2 1/2 lbs Russet Potatoes
- Vegetable or Peanut Oil, for frying
- Sea Salt, for sprinkling

METHOD

1. Heat the heavy cream in a saucepan over medium heat. Add the crumbled blue cheese and whisk until the cheese has melted and the sauce thickens to the desired consistency, about 5 minutes. Remove from heat and add the black pepper and chopped parsley. Set aside and keep warm.

2. Season the steaks with the Big Swede BBQ Badass Beef Boost or your favorite beef rub and let them sit seasoned in room temperature for at least 45 minutes.

3. Peel, rinse, and cut each potato into sticks. Place the fries in a large bowl with cold water and soak for 2 or 3 hours.

4. Pat dry with paper towels.
Heat a few inches of vegetable oil to 300°F or 149°C in a heavy pot. Fry the potatoes for

4-5 minutes in batches. Once all the pota have been fried, turn up the heat until th temperature reaches 400°F or 204°C. Fry potatoes again, cooking until golden and Remove and drain on paper towels. Sprin the fries with sea salt.

5. Prepare grill for direct heat together wi grillgrates. Aim for a grate temperature of 630°F or 332°C.

6. Grill the strip steaks on the grill until reach an inner temperature of 135°F or 57 Flip them every 45 seconds. When ready, remove and rest for 5 minutes.

7. Slice the steaks into thin slices against grain and drizzle with the gorgonzola sau Serve immediately with the French fries.

Foie Gras

WAGYU BURGER

SERVES
2-4

TIME
30 MINS

METHOD
GRILLING

INGREDIENTS

- 1 lb Ground Wagyu
- 1 Tbs Big Swede BBQ Badass Burger Boost
- 4 slices Foie Gras
- 4 Brioche Buns
- 1 Yellow Onion
- 1 Tbs Butter
- Duck Fat Spray
- Red Swiss Chard, stems removed
- Big Swede BBQ Badass Texas Boost

Truffle Aioli:
- 1 large Egg
- 2 Tbs White Truffle Oil
- 1 Tbs Garlic Powder
- 2 Tbs lemon Juice
- 1 tsp White Truffle Salt
- 1 cup Extra Virgin Olive Oil

METHOD

1. Make the aioli by blending egg, truffle oil, lemon juice, garlic powder and olive oil in a blender or with a hand blender until thickened. Add truffle salt, mix, and set aside

2. Mix the ground wagyu beef with the Big Swede BBQ Badass Burger Boost or your favorite umami seasoning. Form into four patties and set aside.

3. Light or set your grill to direct hot heat, about 650°F or 345°C. If using wood or charcoal, use white or red oak.

4. Place a cast iron pan on the grill and melt the butter. Slice the onion into thin slices and cook in the butter until caramelized, about 5 minutes. When ready, remove cast iron pan from the grill.

5. Spray the inside of brioche buns

with the duck fat spray and grill the inside of the buns until nicely browned.

6. Season the burgers lightly with the Big Swede BBQ Badass Texas Boost or your favorite SPG rub. Grill the burgers until they reach in inner temperature of 150°F or 66°C, about 8 minutes. Remove from grill and rest.

7. Place a cast iron pan on the grill and sear the foie gras slices for 30 seconds on each side and then remove from grill.

8. Build the burgers by spreading the lower brioche bun with the truffle aioli. Then place a couple of leaves of the red Swiss chard on top. Next, place one burger patty on each burger and a slice of foie gras. Lastly, top the burger with caramelized onions and the top brioche bun. Serve immediately.

Street Corn Salad with

TRITIP

SERVES
4-6

TIME
15 MINS

METHOD
SMOKING

Long popular in California, the rest of the us are finally falling in love with this flavorful cut

METHOD

1. Set your smoker or grill to 235°F or 113°C. Use cherry wood for a good flavor and color.

2. Trim excess fat and silver skin from the tritip. Season the tritip with the Big Swede BBQ Badass Beef Boost or your favorite beef rub. Let the rub infuse for about 45 minutes.

3. Place the tritip in the smoker and smoke it until the internal temperature reaches 110°F or 43°C, about 60 minutes. Remove from the grill. Place butter on top of the tritip and wrap in foil.

4. While the tritip is smoking, shuck the corn, removing both husks and silks. Oil the corn ears and season with the same BBQ rub used for the tritip. Prepare the Mexican street corn salad by adding the red onion, green onions, red bell pepper, jalapeno peppers, cilantro, avocado, smoked paprika, sour cream and

mayo to bowl. Add the juice from the two limes. Season with salt and pepper.

5. Increase the temperature to 550°F or 288°C on the smoker or grill.

6. Grill the corn ears until charred. When charred and cooked through, remove from the grill and cut the kernels of the corn ears. Mix into the street corn salad. Place salad in serving bowls and crumble cotija cheese on top of each one and finish with some cilantro leaves on top.

7. Remove the tritip from the butter and sear on both sides to achieve nice grill marks. Remove when the internal temperature reaches 135°F or 57°C. Rest for a couple of minutes.

8. Slice the tritip against the grain and serve with the Mexican Street Corn Salad.

235°F, 113°C
45 MINS

INGREDIENTS

- 1 large Tritip
- Big Swede BBQ Badass Beef Boost
- 3 Tbs Butter, unsalted
- 8 Corn Ears
- 1 Red Onion, finely diced
- 8 Green Onions, finely sliced
- 1 Red Bell Pepper, finely diced
- 1 cup Cilantro, chopped
- 2 Jalapenos, finely diced
- 1 Avocado, finely diced
- 2 Limes, juiced
- 2 Tbs Sour Cream
- 4 Tbs Mayonnaise
- 1 tsp Smoked Paprika
- Salt and Pepper to season
- 1/2 cup Cotija Cheese, crumbled
- Cilantro Leaves, for garnish

METHOD

1. Light or set your grill to direct grilling hot-medium (600°F, 315°C). Let the grates get hot for at least 10 minutes.

2. Season the beef tenderloin with the Big Swede BBQ Badass Texas Boost or your favorite SPG rub. Sear the tenderloin roast in the grill on all sides and set aside.

3. Prepare the mushroom mix by placing a cast iron skillet in the grill. Heat up the olive oil in the skillet and add mushrooms and shallot. Cook for 4 to 6 minutes until tender and all liquid is evaporated. Add cognac and cook for 2 to 3 minutes until all liquid is evaporated. Stir in mustard and pepper. Cook 2 to 3 minutes. Add duck liver pate and cook for another 2 minutes. Remove from skillet to medium bowl and let it cool.

4. Lower the temperature on the grill or smoker to 425°F or 218°C.

5. Roll out clingwrap on your cutting board. Lay out the prosciutto slices on the clingwrap in a tight overlapping pattern. Then spread a thin layer of the mushroom mix on top. Place the tenderloin in the center and carefully wrap the plastic wrap around the roast. Set in fridge for 30 minutes.

6. Unfold pastry dough on lightly floured cutting board. Roll pastry out to a rectangle. Remove the roast from the plastic wrap and place in the center of the pastry rectangle. Fold pastry dough neatly around roast. Cut off excess pastry dough and press to seal overlapping edges. Score a decorative pattern with a knife into the pastry roll. Finally, brush the egg wash all over the pastry roll.

7. Place the Beef Wellington in the grill and bake for 35 to 50 minutes or until golden brown or the roast reaches an inner temperature of 135°F or 57°C.

8. While the Beef Wellington is cooking, prepare the red wine reduction sauce. Add the butter and onion in large skillet over medium-high heat and sauté until the onion is golden, about 6 minutes. Add red wine, thyme, maple syrup, and concentrated beef stock to skillet and simmer until mixture is reduced by 2/3, about 10 minutes. Season with salt and pepper and set aside.

9. Transfer Beef Wellington to carving board. Let stand 10 minutes.

10. Carve into slices and serve immediately with the red wine reduction sauce.

INGREDIENTS

- 1 Beef Tenderloin, 2 lbs
- Big Swede BBQ Badass Texas Boost
- 1 tsp Olive Oil
- 8 oz Mushrooms, finely chopped (chanterelle, cremini, or porcini)
- 1 Shallot, finely chopped
- 2 Tbs Cognac
- 2 Tbs Dijon Mustard
- 1 tsp Black Pepper
- 1/4 cup Duck or Chicken Liver Pate
- 1 sheet Frozen Puff Pastry, thawed
- ½ lb Prosciutto, thinly sliced
- 5 Egg Yolks, whisked

Red Wine Reduction Sauce:
- 4 Tbs Butter
- 1 1/2 cups Onion, finely chopped
- 2 cups Dry Red Wine
- 1 tsp Thyme, chopped
- 1 tsp Maple Syrup
- 2 Tbs Concentrated Beef Stock
- Salt and pepper

Grilled Beef

WELLINGTON

SERVES
4–6

TIME
90 MINS

METHOD
GRILLING

When it is offered on the menu at a place that really knows how to cook it, Beef Wellington is always my first choice. The buttery pastry wrapped steak will melt in your mouth and also provide a distinct crunch when it's done right. And cooking the Beef Wellington on the grill adds a beautiful smoky aroma to the dish that really elevates its savory and rich flavors.

INGREDIENTS

- 1 whole Packer Brisket (14-18 lbs)
- 1/2 cup Black Tellicherry Pepper
- 1/2 cup Coarse Sea Salt
- 1/2 cup Big Swede BBQ Badass Beef Boost
- 2 liter Beef Broth

Smoked Beef

BRISKET

SERVES
3-4

TIME
12 HRS

METHOD
SMOKING

METHOD

1. Set your smoker or grill to 235°F or 113°C. If using wood or pellets, use white oak or mesquite.

2. Start by trimming the brisket but don't overdo it though, fat is flavor. Trim and remove the hard, large pieces of fat. They will not render out during the smoke. Leave about ¼ inch of fat on the brisket.

3. Season the brisket with a heavy coating of the Big Swede BBQ Badass Beef Boost or your favorite beef BBQ rub first, then add a second layer of the coarse salt and black pepper. Let the brisket sit at room temperature for an hour to allow the seasoning to set.

4. Pour the beef broth into a large aluminum pan.

5. Place the brisket in the grill on the middle rack with the fat-side towards the heat source and slide the aluminum pan with beef broth underneath. Smoke the brisket until it reaches an internal temperature of 170°F or 77°C.

6. Remove brisket, pour some of the brisket drippings over it and wrap tightly in butcher paper.

7. Place the wrapped brisket back in the grill and cook until it reaches an internal temperature of 204°F or 95°C. Test doneness by probing the brisket with a thermometer – when it feels like it is going into soft butter, then the brisket is done.

8. Remove from grill and let the brisket rest in the butcher paper in a cooler for at least 2 hours.

9. Collect the brisket drippings and the beef broth – separate the fat using an oil separator.

10. When ready to eat, unwrap brisket, slice against the grain and brush slices with the brisket drippings.

POU

Poultry

I have been a certified BBQ judge for many years, and I have found that most of my judging friends are looking forward to the smoked ribs, the smoked pork, or the flavorful smoked brisket the most.

Myself, I am a chicken man!!

I just love the chicken. There is something magical about how you can transform that rather dull piece of meat into a smoky, rich, sweet and flavorful chicken thigh or leg. It blows me away every single time.

And isn't that what backyard cooking is all about? Making something transform, in both texture, flavor and color, when it hits burning coal and wood or kissed by a thin blue smoke. And then having your guests swoon with joy when they take that first bite.

And poultry also spans over so many different kinds of birds. From the white meat birds like turkey and chicken to the red meat birds like duck or ostrich.

And that is the other thing that I love about poultry. You can cook many different kinds of poultry in a multitude of ways. It allows for experimentation and having some fun with your food. Hopefully you will enjoy some of our fun poultry recipes in this section.

LTRY

Smoked
CHICKEN WINGS

SERVES **TIME** **METHOD**
4–6 60 MINUTES SMOKING

INGREDIENTS

- 3 lbs Chicken Wings
- Big Swede BBQ Badass Bird Boost
- 1 1/2 cup Pure Maple Syrup
- 1 cup Hot Sauce
- 2 cups Hot Buffalo Sauce
- 1 Stick Butter

Homemade Ranch Dressing:
- 1/2 cup Mayonnaise
- 1/2 cup Sour cream
- 1/2 cup Buttermilk
- 1 Tbs fresh Dill, finely chopped
- 1 tsp Parsley
- 1 tsp Chives
- 1 tsp Onion Powder
- 2 tsp Garlic Powder
- 1/2 Lemon, squeezed
- Salt and Pepper, to taste

METHOD

1. Pat the chicken wings dry with paper towel to remove the majority of moisture. Separate the flats and the drumettes. Throw away the tips or use for stock. Place wings on a paper towel in the fridge for 3 hours to dry out the skin.

2. Season the chicken wings with the Big Swede BBQ Badass Bird Boost or your favorite chicken wings BBQ rub. Let sit for 45 minutes to allow the rub to adhere to chicken wings.

3. Melt the butter and mix together with the hot sauce, the hot buffalo sauce, and the pure maple syrup and set aside.

4. Whisk together the mayonnaise, sour cream and milk until smooth. Add the spices and whisk until combined. Add the lemon and whisk again. Pour into a jar and chill in the refrigerator until ready to serve.

5. Set the smoker or grill to 350°F or 177°C. If using wood or pellets, use cherry or fruit wood.

6. Place seasoned wings on smoker and allow to cook until internal temperature reaches 155°F or 68°C, about 45 minutes. Flip the wings over after half the time. Remove chicken wings from smoker.

7. Dip chicken wings in sauce mixture. make sure they are coated all over.

8. Place chicken wings back on smoker an continue to cook until reaching an internal temperature of 165°F or 74°C. You can also coat the wings in the sauce again for an extra saucy wing.

9. Remove chicken wings from the grill and serve immediately with the homemade ranch dressing.

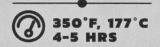

We love spicy and smoky chicken wings and this recipe adds a little sweetness thanks to the smooth maple syrup.

Smokefried
HOT WINGS

SERVES **TIME** **METHOD**
2-4 **90 MINS** **SMOKING &**
FRYING

I like smoked wings. I also like deepfried wings. But I LOVE smokefried wings

INGREDIENTS

- 5 lbs Chicken Wings
- Big Swede BBQ Badass Wing Boost
- Vegetable Oil, for frying

Wing Sauce:
- 12 oz Hot Sauce
- 1 cup BBQ Sauce
- 3/4 cups Maple Syrup
- 1/2 cup Parkay Butter

Blue Cheese Dressing:
- 10 oz Smoked Blue Cheese
- 16 oz Sour Cream
- 1/2 cup Mayonnaise
- 1 Tbs Garlic, minced
- 1/2 Lemon, juiced
- Salt and Pepper

METHOD

1. Separate the flats and drumettes and discard the tips or use for stock. Let the wings sit in the fridge for a couple of hours to dry out the skin.

2. Season richly with the Big Swede BBQ Badass Wing Boost or your favorite wing rub. Let the rub adhere to the chicken wings for an hour.

3. Mix all the ingredients for the blue cheese dressing in a bowl and set aside.

4. Heat up all the ingredients for the wing sauce in a sauce pan over medium heat. Let it simmer for 2 minutes while stirring. Set aside.

5. Set your grill or smoker to 225°F or 107°C. If using wood or pellets, use apple wood.

6. Smoke the chicken for an hour or until they reach an inner temperature of 150°F or 66°C. Flip the wings a couple of times during this part. When ready, remove them from the grill.

7. Pour vegetable oil into your deep fryer and heat it up until the oil reaches 350°F or 177°C.

8. Fry the wings in batches until they have a a beautiful mahogany color and the skin crisps up, about 2-3 minutes per batch. Remove from the fryer and cook the next batch.

9. When all the chicken wings are fried, toss them with the wings sauce and serve immediately with the blue cheese dressing.

225°F (107°C)
90 MINS

Grilled Chicken Souvlaki
PITAS

SERVES	TIME	METHOD
6-8	15 MINS	GRILLING

METHOD

1. Add garlic, oregano, rosemary, paprika, salt, pepper, olive oil, white wine, and lemon juice to a blender. Pulse until well combined.

2. Trim excessive fat of the chicken thighs and cut into 1 1/2-inch pieces. Place the chicken thigh pieces in a large bowl and add the marinade. Toss to combine and make sure the all the chicken pieces are coated with the souvlaki marinade. Cover tightly and refrigerate for 2 hours or preferably overnight

3. Set your grill to direct grilling medium hot heat, 550°F or 288°C. If using wood or pellets, use fruit wood like apple or cherry.

4. Use metal skewers or soak 10 to 12 wooden skewers in water for 45 minutes. When ready, thread the marinated chicken pieces onto the skewers.

5. Place chicken skewers on the grill and grill until nicely browned and they have reached an internal temperature of 165°F or 74°C, about 12-15 minutes. Be sure to rotate the skewers frequently to cook the chicken on all sides. While grilling, brush lightly with the marinade.

6. Prepare the pitas by slicing a pocket in the bread. Add some lettuce to the pocket. Spoon in tomatoes, cucumbers, and red onions.

7. Remove chicken from skewers and add to the pitas. Top with a drizzle of tzatziki and some crumbled feta cheese.

550°F, 288°C
15 MINS

INGREDIENTS

- 2 1/2 Lbs Skinless Chicken Thighs
- 12 Pita Breads
- 3 cups Lettuce,chopped
- 1 cup Tzatziki Sauce
- 3 Tomatoes, chopped
- 2 Cucumber, sliced
- 2 Red Onion, sliced
- 2 cups Feta Cheese, crumbled

Souvlaki Marinade:
- 10 Garlic Cloves, peeled
- 3 Tbsp Dried Oregano
- 2 tsp Dried Rosemary
- 2 tsp Sweet Paprika
- 1 tsp Salt
- 1 tsp Black Pepper
- 1/4 cup Greek Extra Virgin Olive Oil
- 1/4 cup Dry White Wine
- 1 Lemon, juiced

INGREDIENTS

- 3 lbs Chicken Wings
- Big Swede BBQ Badass Texas Boost
- 1 Tbs Toasted Sesame Seeds
- 1 Tbs Green Onion, chopped

Homemade Teriyaki Glaze:
- 2/3 cup Mirin Rice Wine
- 1 cup Soy Sauce
- 2 Tbs Rice Vinegar
- 1/3 Cup Brown Sugar
- 2 tsp Sesame Oil
- 2 Tbs Ginger, minced
- 8 Garlic Cloves, minced
- 3 Tbs Cornstarch
- 3 Tbs Water.

Creamy Sesame Dressing:
- 1/2 cup Mayonnaise
- 1/4 cup Mirin Rice Wine
- 1 Tbs Soy Sauce
- 1 Green Onion, chopped
- 2 Tbs Sesame Oil
- 1/2 tsp Ground Ginger
- 1 tsp Ground Garlic
- 2 Tbs Maple syrup
- 1 tsp Sriracha
- Salt and Pepper, to taste

**225°F, 107°C
60 MINS**

Smoked Teriyaki
CHICKEN WING

SERVES	TIME	METHOD
3-4	60 MINS	SMOKING

METHOD

1. Set your grill or smoker to 225°F or 107°C. If using wood or pellets, use apple wood.

2. Trim the wings into flats and drumettes and season with the Big Swede BBA Badass Texas Boost or your favorite SPG rub.

3. Smoke the wings for about 45 minutes. The wings will still be slightly undercooked.

4. Combine all the ingredients for the teriyaki glace except cornstarch and water in a pan and bring to a low boil. Simmer for 15 minutes. When finished, mix with immersion blender. Add cornstarch to the water and stir until mixed. Add water and cornstarch to the teriyaki glaze, mix well, and stir until thickened. Set aside.

5. Blend all ingredients for the creamy sesame dressing in a blender until smooth. Set aside.

6. After 45 minutes, remove the wings from the grill and increase the temperature to high heat, 650°F or 343°C.

7. Grill the wings for another 8-10 minutes, or until they have an internal temperature of 165°F or 74°C. When ready, remove them from the grill.

8. Toss the wings in the glaze and sprinkle some toasted sesame seeds and sliced green onions on top. Serve immediately with the Creamy Sesame Dressing.

Smoked Chicken
DRUMETTES

SERVES
2-4

TIME
105 MINS

METHOD
SMOKING

INGREDIENTS

- 2 lb Chicken Drumettes
- Big Swede BBQ Badass Bird Boost
- 1 cup BBQ Sauce
- 3 sticks Butter, sliced
- 2 Tbs Maple Syrup
- 2 Tbs Apple Juice

**300°F, 149°C
105 MINS**

METHOD

1. Pull back the skin on the chicken leg and remove the tendons underneath and trim off some of the silverskin. Then fold the skin back over the leg again.

2. Season the chicken legs generously with the Big Swede BBQ Badass Bird Boost or your favorite poultry rub.

3. Place the chicken legs in an aluminum pan and place 2 sticks of the butter slices both under and top of the chicken legs.

4. Set your grill or smoker to 300°F or 149°C. If using wood or pellets, use apple or cherry wood.

5. Place the aluminum pan on an elevated rack and smoke the chicken legs

for an hour.

6. Mix the last stick of the butter with the BBQ sauce, apple juice, and maple syrup in a saucepan over medium heat.

7. Foil the pan and place back in the smoker. Steam the chicken legs for 30 minutes or until they reach an inner temperature of 190°F or 88°C.

8. Remove the chicken legs from the pan and place back on the grill for about 5 minutes.

9. Remove the legs from the grill and dip them in the sauce. Place them back in the smoker for the last time and smoke for another 10 minutes and then they are ready to serve.

Smoked
TURKEY BREAST

SERVES
4–6

TIME
4–5 HRS

METHOD
SMOKING

INGREDIENTS

- 1 Turkey Breast,
  whole with skin
- Big Swede BBQ
  Badass Bird Boost
- 2 sticks Butter
- Duckfat spray

Turkey Brine:
- 9 cups Water
- 1/2 cup Salt
- 1/2 cup Sugar
- 5 cloves Garlic,
  crushed and peeled
- 3 sprigs Rosemary
- 5 sprigs Thyme
- 1 Lemon, sliced
- 2 tsp Peppercorns
- 2 Bay Leaves

**350°F, 177°C
4-5 HRS**

I prefer turkey breast to whole turkey, it smokes better and it is easier to carve.

METHOD

1. In 6-quart container or stockpot, mix water, salt and sugar. Stir until sugar and salt are dissolved. Add the rest of the ingredients for the brine. Then add the turkey breast and cover. Refrigerate at least 12 hours but no longer than 24 hours.

2. Rinse brine from turkey breast. Pat dry and let it sit in the fridge for 6 hours to dry out the skin.

3. Let butter soften up in a bowl at room temperature and then mix in 3 Tbs of the Big Swede BBQ Badass Bird Boost or your favorite poultry rub.

4. Spread the seasoned butter all over the turkey breast. Also smear some seasoned butter inside the turkey cavity and add plenty of seasoned butter between the skin and the turkey meat as well.

5. Spray the turkey breast lightly with duckfat to get the rub to adhere better to the skin. Season the turkey breast on all sides with the Big Swede BBQ Badass Bird Boost or your favorite poultry rub. Also season

the inside cavity with the rub.

6. Set your smoker or grill to 350°F or 177°C. If using wood or pellets, use apple or peach wood.

7. Place the turkey breast in the smoker on an elevated rack to ensure good airflow all around the bird.

8. Smoke the turkey breast for 2-3 hours until it reaches an inner temperature of 145°F or 63°C. Spray with additional duckfat every 30 minutes to keep the turkey breast moist.

9. Increase the temperature on the smoker to 400°F or 204°C.

10. Continue to smoke the turkey breast until it reaches an inner temperature of 160°F or 71°C.

11. Wrap turkey breast in heavy-duty aluminum foil, then wrap in several layers of thick towels, and allow to rest for about 45 minutes. The residual heat will finish cooking the turkey breast to a safe temperature of 165°F or 74°C.

Grilled Chicken
ROCHAMBEAU

SERVES	TIME	METHOD
8-10	60 MIN	GRILLING

METHOD

1. Marinate the chicken breast fillets in the Mojo Marinade for at least 4 hours, preferably overnight in the refrigerator.

2. To make the Marchand sauce, melt the butter in a large sauté pan over low heat and gradually add the flour stirring constantly. Continue cooking over low heat for 10 minutes until the roux is light brown.

3. Next, add the ham, green onions, mushrooms, onions and garlic to the roux. Cook and stir for 5 minutes.
Add the beef stock and red wine, while continuing to stir. Lower the temperature to very low heat and continue to cook for 30 minutes while stirring every 5 minutes.

4. To make the hollandaise sauce, melt the butter in a pan. Add the egg yolks, lemon juice, Dijon mustard, turmeric, and salt into a blender and blend for 5 seconds until combined. With the blender running on medium high, slowly stream in the hot butter into the mixture until it's emulsified.

5. Remove the chicken breast slices from the marinade. Pat them dry and season on both sides the Big Swede BBQ Badass Bird Boost or your favorite poultry rub.

6. Set up your grill or smoker to 550°F or 288°C. If using wood or pellets, use pecan or maple wood. wrap.

7. Spray both sides of your bread slices with Duck Fat Spray and grill until lightly grilled with visible sear marks. Flip the bread and lightly grill the other side. Remove and keep it warm.

8. Place the ham and chicken fillets on the grill. Grill the ham slices until thoroughly heated with good sear marks, about one minute per side. Grill the chicken breast fillets on both sides until the inner temperature reaches 165°F or 74°C.

9. Assemble by first ladling the Marchand de Vin sauce on a plate. Next, place the bread centered on top the sauce. Then layer a slice of ham followed by a chicken breast fillet on top of the bread. Spoon some of the Hollandaise sauce on top of the chicken and finish by sprinkling the sandwich with a garnish of chopped chives. Serve immediately.

INGREDIENTS

- Chicken Breast, cut in 1/2-inch thick fillets
- Big Swede BBQ Badass Bird Boost
- 2 cups Mojo Marinade
- Artisan French bread, sliced
- Duck Fat Spray
- Smoked Ham, sliced into 1/8-inch thick slices
- Chives, finely chopped

Hollandaise Sauce:
- 3 Egg Yolks
- 1 Tbs Lemon Juice
- 1 tsp Dijon Mustard
- 1/2 tsp Salt
- 1/2 cup Ghee
- 1 tsp Turmeric, for color

Marchand de vin sauce:
- 1 stick Unsalted Butter
- 3 Tbs Flour
- 1/2 Cup Baked Ham, very finely chopped
- 1/3 Cup Green Onions, very finely chopped
- 3/4 Cup Cremini Mushrooms, very finely chopped
- 1/2 Onion, very finely chopped
- 4 Garlic Cloves, minced
- 1 tsp Salt
- 1 tsp Black Pepper
- 4 cups Beef Stock
- 2/3 Cup Cabernet Sauvignon

Wild Mushroom Ragu with

PHEASANT

SERVES | **TIME** | **METHOD**
2–4 | 60 MINS | DIRECT GRILLING

INGREDIENTS

- 2 whole Pheasants
- 2 cups Herbed Butter (Sage, Rosemary, Thyme)

Pheasant Brine:
- 1/4 cup Kosher Salt
- 1/4 cup Brown Sugar
- 4 cups Water
- 10 Black Pepper Corns
- 4 Bay Leaves

Wild Mushroom Ragu:
- 1 tsp Extra Virgin Olive Oil
- 1/4 lb Pancetta, coarsely chopped
- 1 1/2 lbs Chanterelles, Porcini, and Shiitake Mushrooms
- 1 large Shallot, finely chopped
- 1 tsp Thyme, finely chopped
- 1/4 cup Madeira Wine
- 1/4 cup Beef or Veal Reduction
- 3/4 cup Heavy Cream
- Salt and Pepper, to taste

Rustic pheasant is delicious with rich and earthy mushrooms

METHOD

1. Dissolve the salt and sugar in the water and add the peppercorns and bay leaves. Find a lidded container just about large enough to hold both pheasants.

2. Cover the pheasant in the brine and let the container sit in the fridge for at least 12 hours and up to 18 hours.

3. Take the pheasants out of the brine. Set in a breezy place and let them dry for an hour or so. This drying process is an important step to avoid rubbery skin.

4. Cut the pheasants in half and rub with the herbed butter thoroughly. Try to get some under the skin as well. Reserve half of the herbed butter for basting.

5. Set upp your grill or smoker to 375°F or 190°C and if you are using pellets or wood, choose a fruit wood like Apple or Cherry.

6. Place the pheasants skin side down and cook for 30 minutes. Baste every 10 minutes. Then turn the pheasants skin side up and continue roasting and basting until you reach

an inner temperature in the thigh of 160°F or 71°C.

7. While the pheasant is roasting, prepare the wild mushroom ragu. In a large deep skillet, heat the olive oil. Add the pancetta and cook over moderately high heat while stirring, until golden, about 5 minutes. Using a slotted spoon, transfer the pancetta to a plate, leave the fat in the skillet.

8. Add the mushrooms to the skillet and cook over moderately high heat, stirring occasionally, until lightly browned and softened, about 8 minutes. Add the shallot and thyme and cook until the shallot is softened. Add the Madeira and the beef or veal reduction and cook until evaporated, scraping up any browned bits on the bottom of the skillet. Stir in the cream, season with salt and pepper and simmer until the ragout is slightly thickened, 2 to 3 minutes.

9. Just before serving, stir in the pancetta and stir carefully.

10. Remove the pheasants from the grill and let them rest for 5 minutes. Serve the pheasants with the wild mushroom ragu.

Mexican Escabeche and
POLLO ASADO

SERVES
4–6

TIME
15 MINS

METHOD
GRILLING

Pollo Asado is Mexican grilled chicken that's been marinated in a mixture of citrus juices, spices, and achiote paste, which gives the chicken its signature orange and red color

METHOD

1. Bring 1/2 quart of water to a boil and add the peeled and sliced carrots. Boil the carrots for 5 minutes.

2. Add onion, jalapenos, oregano, garlic, apple cider vinegar, vegetable oil, bay leaves and salt. Boil for 2 more minutes. Remove from the burner and cool for a couple of hours. Place in a jar overnight.

3. Place all the ingredients in the pollo asado marinade in a blender and blend on high.

4. Trim the chicken quarters and remove all excess fat. Place the chicken quarters in an aluminum pan. Pour the pollo asado marinade over the chicken quarters and mix thoroughly. Ensure that all the chicken quarters are coated in the marinade.

5. Place the marinated chicken in the refrigerator overnight.

6. Heat your grill or smoker to 375°F or 190°C. If using wood or pellets, use mesquite wood.

7. Remove the chicken quarters from the marinade and place on the grill. Grill bone side down first for 5-6 minutes. Flip the chicken quarters and grill them skin side down for another 3-4 minutes. Baste them with some of the marinade. Then continue flipping and basting the chicken quarters every 90 seconds until they reach in inner temperature of 165°F or 74°C.

8. Remove the chicken quarters from the grill and let them rest for a couple of minutes.

9. Serve the Grilled Pollo Asado with the Mexican Escabeche.

INGREDIENTS

- 4 Chicken Quarters

Asado Marinade:
- 1 Garlic Head
- 2 Tbs Achiote Paste
- 2 Chipotle Peppers in Adobo Sauce
- 1 tsp Cumin
- 1 tsp Allspice
- 1 tsp Black Pepper
- 2 tsp Oregano
- 3 tsp Sea Salt
- 3 Oranges, juiced
- 3 Limes, juiced
- 1/2 cup Extra Virgin Olive Oil

Mexican Escabeche:
- 1/2 quart Water
- 3 large Carrots, peeled and sliced
- 1 Yellow Onion, sliced
- 4 Jalapenos, deseeded and sliced
- 1 Tbs Oregano
- 6 Garlic Cloves, sliced
- 1 cup Apple Cider Vinegar
- 1/4 cup Vegetable Oil
- 2 Bay Leaves
- 1 tsp Sea Salt

**375°F (190°C)
15 MINS**

Chicken and Sausage
JAMBALAYA

SERVES	TIME	METHOD
8-10	90 MIN	GRILLING

METHOD

1. Set up your grill or smoker to 425°F or 218°C. If using wood or pellets, use pecan or maple wood.

2. Trim and season the chicken thighs with Creole seasoning. Place the chicken thighs, the Kielbasa and Andouille sausages, and the tomatoes on the grill.

3. Grill the chicken until it reaches an internal temperature of 165°F or 74°C, about 20 minutes. Cook sausages until nicely browned, about 10 minutes. Grill the tomatoes until they have grill marks and start to blacken, about 5 minutes. Remember to turn chicken and sausage occasionally.

4. Transfer chicken, sausage, and tomatoes to a cutting board as they are done. When cool enough to handle, pull chicken into large chunks, slice the sausages, and chop the tomatoes.

5. Place a large cast iron pan in the grill. Add the olive oil to the pan and heat until shimmering. Add onions, pepper, and celery and cook until vegetables have softened, 7 to 8 minutes, and stir occasionally. Add the bacon and cook for about 10 minutes until nicely browned. Add garlic, the Big Swede BBQ Badass Texas Boost or your favorite SPG rub, and hot sauce and cook for 2 minutes.

6. Add rice and stir to thoroughly coat grains with the mixture. Add chicken stock and bay leaf. Simmer until rice is fully cooked, 20-30 minutes.

7. Stir in chicken, sausage and tomatoes and heat cook until heated through, 3 to 5 minutes.

8. Season again if needed with Big Swede BBQ Badass Texas Boost to taste. Plate the Jambalaya and top with green onions. Serve immediately.

425°F, 218°C
90 MINS

INGREDIENTS

- 2 lbs Chicken Thighs
- 1 Tbs Creole Seasoning
- 1 lb Kielbasa Sausage
- 1/2 lb Andouille
- 2 Roma Tomatoes, halved
- 2 Tbs Extra Virgin Olive Oil
- 1 Yellow Onion, finely diced
- 1 Green Pepper, finely diced
- 1 Celery Stalk, finely diced
- 1/2 lb Bacon or Ham, diced
- 5 Garlic Cloves, minced
- 1 Tbs Big Swede BBQ Badass Texas Boost
- 2 tsp Hot sauce
- 3/4 cup White Rice
- 3 cups Chicken Broth
- 2 Bay Leafs
- 1/2 cup Green Onions, finely sliced

Orange Endive Salad with Smoked Moulard
DUCK BREAST

SERVES
2-4

TIME
60 MINS

METHOD
SMOKING

The Moulard Duck is often referred to as the "ribeye in the sky" and tastes like a premium steak with a rich duck flavor twist.

INGREDIENTS

- **Moulard Duck Breast**
- **Big Swede BBQ Badass Texas Boost**

Orange Endive Salad:
- 2 heads Belgian Endive
- 1/2 cup Walnut halves, toasted
- 1/4 lb Roquefort Cheese, crumbled
- 1/2 cup Baby Arugula
- 1/2 cup Baby Spinach
- 1 cup Frisée Leaves
- 2 Oranges
- Mustard Vinaigrette

METHOD

1. Score the skin of the Moulard Duck Breast in a tight pattern. Be careful not to cut into the meat. Season both sides of duck breast with the Big Swede BBQ Badass Texas Boost or your favorite SPG rub.

2. Set your grill or smoker to 225°F or 107°C. If using wood or pellets, use apple wood.

3. Place the duck breast fat side up in the grill and smoke until the duck breast reaches an inner temperature of 120°F or 49°C.

4. Remove the duck breast from the grill and increase the temperature to 600°F or 315°C. Now place the duck breast fat side down and sear the fat side for a couple of minutes. Move the duck breast around to avoid burning from the flare ups when the fat hits the grill.

The duck breast is finished when the inner temperature hits 130°F or 55°C. Let the duck breast rest for 5 minutes while you make the salad.

5. Separate the endive leaves and cut the leaves in half lengthwise. Place in a large bowl together with the baby arugula, baby spinach, and frisée leaves.

6. Drizzle with the mustard vinaigrette and toss gently. Then, add the toasted walnuts and plate the salad.

7. Add some crumbled Roquefort cheese to the plate. Peel the oranges and cut into orange supremes. Add the orange supremes to salad.

8. Slice the duck breast thinly and place slices on the plated salad. Serve immediately.

225°F, 107°C
60 MINS

Grilled Lemon-Thyme
CHICKEN BREAST

SERVES	TIME	METHOD
4-6	15 MINS	GRILLING

The key to grilling chicken breast is to trim it to equal thickness across and flip it frequently on the grill to ensure an even cook

METHOD

1. Finely chop thyme and then mix thyme, vinaigrette, mustard, olive oil, garlic, salt and pepper in a bowl. Pour mixture over chicken and let marinate overnight.

2. Whisk lemon juice, olive oil, mustard, agave, and dill in a medium bowl then add tomatoes, cucumber, and feta cheese. Toss gently, season to taste then refrigerate at least an hour before serving.

3. Season the salad with the Big Swede BBQ Badass Veggie Boost or your favorite herb seasoning for vegetables.

4. Set up your grill or smoker

to 550°F or 288°C. If using wood or pellets, use pecan or maple wood. wrap.

5. Remove the chicken breasts from the marinade and place them on the grill.

6. Grill the chicken breast 12–15 minutes, turning often, until they reach an inner temperature of 165°F or 74°C.

7. Grill lemon slices a couple of minutes on each side until they have good sear marks.

8. Slice chicken and serve with lemon slices and the feta salad. Serve immediately.

550°F, 288°C
15 MINS

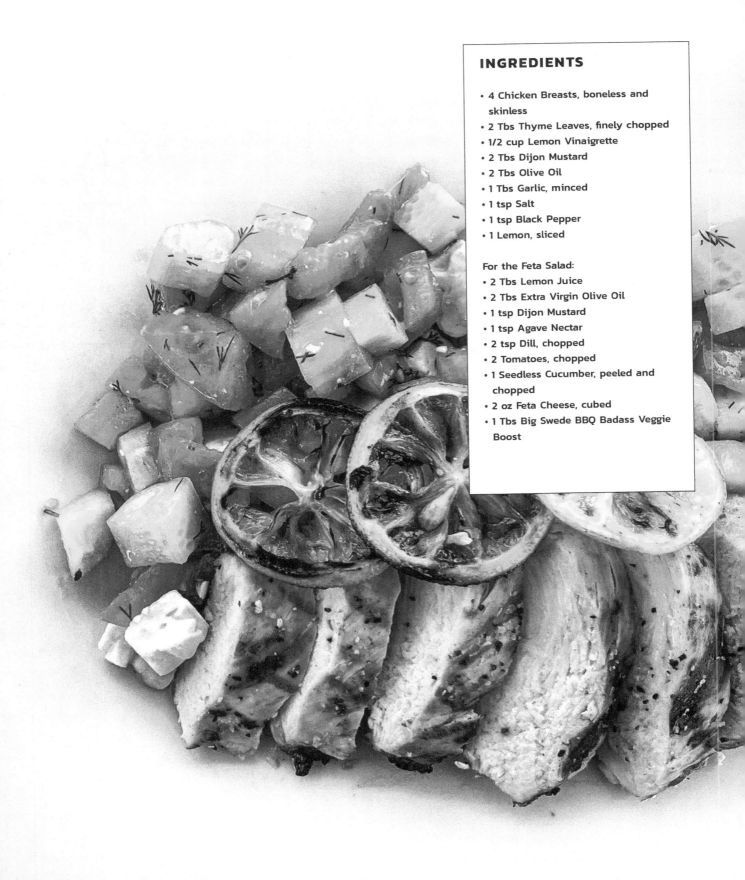

INGREDIENTS

- 4 Chicken Breasts, boneless and skinless
- 2 Tbs Thyme Leaves, finely chopped
- 1/2 cup Lemon Vinaigrette
- 2 Tbs Dijon Mustard
- 2 Tbs Olive Oil
- 1 Tbs Garlic, minced
- 1 tsp Salt
- 1 tsp Black Pepper
- 1 Lemon, sliced

For the Feta Salad:
- 2 Tbs Lemon Juice
- 2 Tbs Extra Virgin Olive Oil
- 1 tsp Dijon Mustard
- 1 tsp Agave Nectar
- 2 tsp Dill, chopped
- 2 Tomatoes, chopped
- 1 Seedless Cucumber, peeled and chopped
- 2 oz Feta Cheese, cubed
- 1 Tbs Big Swede BBQ Badass Veggie Boost

Smoked
SPATCHCOCK CHICKEN

SERVES
2–4

TIME
90 MINS

METHOD
SMOKING

You can also use this recipe for turkey or other poultry as well. The spatchcock technique helps cook any bird faster and more evenly.

INGREDIENTS

- 1 Whole Chicken
- Big Swede BBQ Badass Bird Boost
- 1 stick Butter
- Duck Fat Spray

Chicken Brine:
- 2 quarts Water
- 1/3 cup Kosher Salt
- 2 Lemons, quartered
- 10 sprigs Parsley
- 10 sprigs Thyme
- 3 sprigs Rosemary
- 3 Bay leaves
- 1/2 cup Honey
- 6 Garlic Cloves, smashed
- 15 Black Peppercorns

METHOD

1. Mix all the ingredients for the brine in a large stockpot and completely submerse the chicken. Brine for 4 hours then remove chicken from brine, rinse and pat dry.

2. Let the chicken sit uncovered in the fridge for about 2 hours to allow the skin to dry out a little.

3. To spatchcock the chicken, begin by cutting out the backbone. Open the chicken by breaking the breastbone and then flatten the chicken and tuck the wings under the spatchcock chicken.

4. Preheat your smoker or grill and set it up for smoking to 350°F or 177°C. If using wood or pellets, use apple or cherry wood.

5. Mix the butter with 2 Tbs of the Big Swede BBQ Badass Bird Boost or your favorite chicken rub. Gently stick your hand under the skin and stuff some of the butter mix under the skin of each breast, creating an even layer. Use the same rub, and season both sides of the chicken.

6. Place the chicken in the grill or smoker and cook for 90 minutes or until the breast reaches an inner temperature of 165°F or 74°C

7. Baste with duckfat spray or melted butter every 20 minutes. When ready the skin should be golden and crispy.

8. Remove the spatchcock chicken from the smoker and let it rest for 5 minutes then serve immediately.

**350°F, 177°C
90 MINS**

INGREDIENTS

- 8 Quails
- Big Swede BBQ Badass Veggie Boost
- Duckfat Spray

Foie Gras Sauce:
- 2 slices Foie Gras
- 1 Shallot, finely shopped
- 1 sprig Thyme
- 2 Tbs Butter
- 1 cup Malbec Wine
- 2 cups Beef Stock
- 1 cup Heavy Cream
- Salt and Pepper, to taste

Foie Gras Sauce and
GRILLED QUAILS

SERVES
3-4

TIME
15 MIN

METHOD
GRILLING

METHOD

1. Melt the butter in a saucepan over medium-high heat. Add the finely chopped shallots and sauté for 3 minutes until translucent.

2. Deglaze the pan with the wine and cook until reduced to half. Add the thyme sprig and the beef broth and reduce to a third. Remove the thyme sprig.

3. Lower the temperature to low-medium and add the heavy cream. Also crumble the foie gras slices into the sauce and slowly cook until the foie gras is completely melted into the sauce. Don't boil the sauce because then it will break. Season with salt and pepper. Set aside and keep warm.

4. Set up your grill or smoker to 550°F or 288°C. If using wood or pellets, use pecan or maple wood.

5. Next, spatchcock the quails. Use kitchen shears to cut out the backbones of the quail, then flatten them with your hands so they cook evenly.

6. Spray both sides of the quails with duck fat and then season with the Big Swede BBQ Badass Veggie Boost or your favorite herb poultry rub.

7. Place the quails on the grill breast side up and cook until the quails have an inner temperature of 155° or 68°C.

8. Flip them over and quickly sear the breast to get some charred flavor and nice grill marks. Remove from the grill and rest for 3 minutes.

9. Place the quails on a place and drizzle with the foie gras sauce. Serve immediately.

INGREDIENTS

- 1 whole Duck
- 1 lb Kosher Salt

Duck Glaze:
- 4 Tbs Orange Juice
- 4 Tbs Agave Nectar
- 3 Tbs Soy Sauce
- 2 Tbs Mirin Rice Wine
- 2 Tbs Dry Sherry
- 1 Tbs Big Swede BBQ Badass Wing Boost
- 1 Tbs BBQ Sauce

Smoked Asian
DUCK

SERVES
3–4

TIME
4 HRS

METHOD
SMOKING

Smoked Duck is delicious and this recipe helps render out the fat, makes the skin cripsy, and packs the fresh duck full of asian flavors

METHOD

1. Pierce the skin of the duck, but don't pierce through the meat. Sprinkle the duck with Kosher salt and brine overnight.

2. Bring a large pan filled with water to a boil. When boiling – pour the water over the duck to wash away the salt. The boiling water helps render some of the fat. Pat dry and let it sit in room temperature for 30 minutes.

3. Light or set your smoker or grill to 300°F or 149°C. If using wood or pellets, use maple or pecan wood.

4. Mix all the ingredients for the glaze in a sauce pan over medium heat. Simmer for 2 minutes and then set aside.

5. Place the duck in the smoker. Brush the duck with the sauce to glaze it every 30 minutes. Smoke and baste the duck for 3 hours

or until the internal temperature reaches 160°F or 71°C.

6. Remove the duck from the smoker and let it rest under some aluminum foil.

7. Increase the temperature on the grill or smoker to 500°F or 260°C.

8. Place the duck back in the smoker and crips the skin for 8-10 minutes while basting every 4 minutes. The internal temperature should be 165°F or 74°C.

9. Remove the duck from the smoker and let it rest for 10 minutes.

10. Carve the duck into 1/2-inch slices. If you have any duck glaze left, heat it up again and serve together with the sliced duck.

Pork

I didn't eat a lot of pork growing up. Or at least not a lot of great pork. We had an occasional pork roast and sometimes we ate some grilled pork chops. But I don't recall any of those dinners being very memorable. And to make things worse, there was the infamous Flintastek.

During the summertime we often had something called "Flintasteak" (translates into Flintstone steaks), a horrible Swedish creation, made with a fresh pork ham that was sliced into 1-inch slices and then marinated for days in an oily marinade. We would buy these pre-marinated Flintasteks in the local grocery stores and then char them beyond recognition on disposable charcoal grills that were lit with lighter fuel. And every single Swede I know, have had this terrible food experience during their childhood. So, growing up, I wasn't really impressed by pork. To be honest, I did not like it at all.

And then you get to taste ribs smoked over low heat and glazed with a beautiful Kansas City-style rib glaze. Or you get to experience a perfectly smoked money muscle from the pork butt at a BBQ competition. Or you try Iberico Bellota Secretos, seasoned only with sea salt and grilled over oak wood fire.

And your life changes. And you suddenly see the greatness in pork.

PORK

Smoked Babyback

SWEET RIBS

SERVES
5–6

TIME
6 HRS

METHOD
SMOKING

Who doesn't love juicy and tender babyback ribs with a little bit of heat and a little bit of sweet?

METHOD

1. Remove the end bones from each slab of ribs to give a square appearance. Trim any excess fat from the ribs and pull the membrane off the backside of the ribs.

2. Season both sides of the ribs with a good dusting of the Big Spade BBQ Badass Pork Boost or your favorite sweet BBQ rub. Let the ribs sweat for 45 minutes to infuse the rub with the meat.

3. Set your smoker to 235°F or 113°C. If using wood or pellets, use cherry wood for good flavor and color.

4. Place the ribs in the grill and cook for 2 hours. Spritz with Apple Juice every 30 minutes. When the ribs reach a mahogany color and the bark is set, remove them from the smoker.

5. Place each rib on two sheets of aluminum foil. Layer butter, brown sugar, and agave nectar on the foil. Place a slab of ribs meat side up and sprinkle butter, brown sugar and agave nectar on top. Add a

tablespoon of peach nectar to the foil as well. Close the foil carefully and repeat for the other slabs.

6. Place the wrapped ribs back on the grill and continue to cook for 2 hours or until tender. Be sure to check the ribs for tenderness at the 90-minute mark.

7. When a few of the larger bones are exposed on the back and the slab bends easily when lifted the ribs are ready to come off the grill. Also check with a probe – when the probe goes into the meat between the bones like in hot butter, they are ready for saucing. Open the foil and let the ribs steam for a couple of minutes. Inner temperature should be around 202°F or 95°C.

8. Mix the ingredients for the BBQ Sauce.

9. Coat the ribs on both side with the BBQ Sauce and place them back in the grill for a last time. Let the sauce set for 5-10 minutes. Remove the ribs from the grill. Rest for 5 minutes before serving.

INGREDIENTS

- 3 racks Babyback Pork Ribs
- Big Swede BBQ Badass Pork Boost
- Parkay Butter
- Agave Nectar
- Brown Sugar
- Peach Nectar
- Apple Juice, in a spritzer

BBQ Sauce:
- 2 cups Sweet BBQ Sauce
- 1 Cup Agave Nectar
- 1/2 cup Apple Juice

Iberico Pluma with Cherry
CHIMICHURRI

INGREDIENTS

- 2 Iberico Plumas
- Big Swede BBQ Badass Texas Boost

Cherry Chimichurri:
- 1 1/2 cup Cherries
- 2 Shallots, finely chopped
- 1 Jalapeno, deseeded and finely chopped
- 1 small bunch Cilantro
- 1 small bunch Parsley
- 1 small bunch Oregano
- 2 Tbs Red Wine Vinegar
- 1 Tbs Black Cherry Juice
- 1 Tbs Big Swede BBQ Badass Veggie Boost
- 7 Tbs Extra Virgin Olive Oil
- Sea Salt

SERVES	TIME	METHOD
2-3	10 MINS	GRILLING

METHOD

1. Trim the plumas and remove excess fat and any silverskin.

2. Season generously with the Big Swede BBQ Badass Texas Boost or your favorite SPG rub. Let the plumas sit for at least 45 minutes to allow the rub to infuse with the meat.

3. Light or set your grill to direct hot heat, about 650°F or 345°C. If using wood or charcoal, use fruit wood like cherry, peach or apple.

4. Pit and finely chop all the cherries and then place them in a bowl.

5. Finely chop the cilantro, parsley and oregano and add to the bowl.

6. Add the shallots, jalapeno, vinegar, cherry juice and the Big Swede BBQ Badass Veggie Boost or your favorite herb seasoning to the bowl and mix gently.

7. Add the olive oil gradually to the bowl by whisking continuously until emulsified. Set aside and keep cool.

8. When the grill grates are hot, place the plumas on the grill. Grill the plumas for 7-10 minutes until they reach an inner temperature of 155°F or 68°C. Turn the plumas every minute to get a good char all around.

9. When ready, remove the plumas from the grill and let rest for 5 minutes.

10. Slice the plumas against the grain and serve immediately with the cherry chimichurri.

650°F, 345°C
10 MINS

Pluma translates to "feather" due to its wing-like shape. It is very tender and juicy, and considered the most authentic flavor of acorn fed Iberico pig.

SMOKED HAM

SERVES
4–6

TIME
3 1/2 HRS

METHOD
SMOKING

The Maple Bourbon glaze in this recipe is so good it will elevate almost any pork or poultry dish

METHOD

1. Preheat your smoker or grill and set it up for smoking to 250°F or 121°C. If using wood or pellets, use apple or cherry wood.

2. Smear the ham with yellow mustard as a binding agent for the rub. Gently season the ham with the Big Swede BBQ Badass Pork Boost or your favorite pork rub and let sit while the smoker is heating up.

3. Place the ham inside the grill and smoke until the ham reaches an internal temperature of 120°F or 49°C. If the ham looks dry in certain areas, spray it with the apple juice.

4. While the ham is smoking, make the maple bourbon glaze. Add the butter, brown sugar, maple syrup, bourbon whiskey, BBQ sauce and fruit preserve to a cast iron pan.

5. Place the pan in the grill and heat up the glaze. Stir occasionally. Smoking the glaze will give it a nice and light smoke flavor.

6. When the ham reaches 120°F, remove it from the grill and place it in an aluminum pan. Baste the ham generously with the glaze and place it back in the grill. Now continue smoking it until the internal temperature reaches 140°F or 60°C.

7. Baste the ham with more glaze every 15-20 minutes.

8. When the ham is finished, remove it from the grill and let it rest for 15-20 minutes. Slice the ham and serve it with the glaze from aluminum pan.

INGREDIENTS

- 10 lb Hickory Smoked Spiral Ham
- Yellow Mustard
- Big Swede BBQ Badass Pork Boost
- 2 Tbs Butter
- 1/2 cup Brown Sugar
- 1/2 cup Maple Syrup
- 1/2 cup Bourbon Whisky
- 1/2 cup BBQ Sauce
- 2 Tbs Fruit Preserve (Apricot, Sweet Orange or Peach)
- Apple Juice

250°F, 121°C
3 1/2 HRS

INGREDIENTS

- 4 lb Pork Belly, skinless boneless
- Black Tellicherri Pepper

Bacon Cure:
- 4 Tbs Kosher Salt
- 1/2 cup White Sugar
- 2 Tbs Black Pepper
- 1/2 Tbs White Pepper
- 2 tsp Paprika
- 1 1/2 tsp Pink Curing Salt

Smoked and Peppered
BACON

SERVES **TIME** **METHOD**
8-10 **6 HRS** **SMOKING**

Homemade and smoked bacon is so much better than the store bought ones.

METHOD

1. In a small bowl, make the cure by combining all the ingredients for the bacon cure and stir thoroughly.

2. Place belly on a foil lined tray and pat dry with paper towels. Trim off extra thick layers of fat if needed.

3. Use half of the cure mix and sprinkle evenly over the surface of the belly. Rub it in gently and the turn the pork belly over and repeat on other side with remaining mix. Make sure to thoroughly coat all sides of the pork belly and use all of the cure.

4. Place the pork belly with the curing mix into a large zip top bag and place in refrigerator for 7 days. Seal the bag tightly, removing as much air as possible.

5. Flip and massage the pork belly once per day. The curing mix will liquify after some day and this is normal.

6. Remove the pork belly from the bag and rinse it to remove any slimy surface build-up. Place it on a rack over an aluminum pan. Pat the pork belly dry with paper towels. Season the top side heavily with the black Tellichery Pepper or your preferred bacon seasoning.

7. Place the pork belly in the fridge and leave uncovered for 12-24 hours.

8. Set your smoker or grill to 160°F or 71°C. If using wood or pellets, use apple wood. Place the pork belly on an elevated rack with an aluminum pan underneath and smoke for 6 hours, or until the internal temperature of the pork belly reads 155°F or 68°C.

9. Let the pork belly chill completely in the refrigerator before slicing. Slice the pork belly and cook the bacon the way you like it.

160°F (71°C)
6 HRS

INGREDIENTS

- 2 racks Spare Ribs, St. Louis cut
- Big Swede BBQ Badass Texas Boost
- Tellicherry Pepper
- Apple Cider Vinegar, for spritzing
- Butter

Texas Glaze:
- 1 cup BBQ Sauce
- 1 cup Apple Cider Vinegar

Smoked Texas
SPARE RIBS

SERVES
4–6

TIME
6 HRS

METHOD
SMOKING

METHOD

1. Remove the membranes from the back of ribs and the trim off any excess fat.

2. Season the ribs on both sides with the Big Swede BBQ Badass Texas Boost or your favorite SPG rub. Pat the meat to ensure that the rub adheres to the meat. Wait 10 minutes, then season with a layer of the black tellicherry pepper and pat the meat again. Let is sit for 35 minutes.

3. Set your smoker or grill to 275°F or 125°C. If using wood or pellets, use mesquite or oak wood.

4. Smoke the ribs for 3 hours and spritz them every 30 minutes with the apple cider vinegar.

5. Make the Texas glaze by mixing together a good commercial BBQ sauce with the apple cider vinegar.

6. When the seasoning is set on the ribs and they have a nice brown color, with an internal temperature of 170°F or 77°C, remove them from the grill.

7. Glaze both sides with the Texas glaze and place a few slices of butter on top of the ribs. Doublewrap the ribs in butcher paper and place back in the smoker again..

8. Cook for another 1.5 hours or until probe tender and the ribs have an internal temperature of 205°F or 96°C

9. When ribs are done, remove from the smoker and vent the ribs to remove steam for 5 minutes. Refoil, glaze some more if needed and rest for 30 – 45 minutes.

Grilled Swedish "Flintastek" aka

FLINTSTONE STEAK

SERVES	TIME	METHOD
4-6	45 MINS	SMOKING

Flintstone steaks or "Flintastek" could be bought pre-marinated from the grocery stores and was extremely popular to throw on the grill when I was growing up. The name was just a marketing gimmick to sell more ham cuts during the summer.

METHOD

1. Get your butcher to slice a fresh ham into one-inch slices across the bone.

2. Brush the ham slices with vegetable oil and then season richly with our Big Swede BBQ Badass Beef Boost or your favorite BBQ rub.

3. Vaccum seal the seasoned slices or place them in resealable plastic bags and extract as much air as you can from the bags. Let them sit in the fridge for 3 days to allow the seasoning to really infuse with the flintstone steaks.

4. Preheat your smoker or grill and set to 250°F or 121°C. If using wood or pellets, use apple or cherry wood.

5. Place the flintstone steaks in the smoker and smoke until they reach an inner temperature of 115°F or 46°C, about 45 minutes.

6. Remove the flintstone steaks from the grill and wrap them in aluminum foil.

7. Increase the temperature of the grill to 600°F or 315°C. When the grates are hot, sear both sides of the flintstone steaks on the grill. Remove them when they reach an inner temperature of 145°F or 63°C

8. Let the steaks rest for 5 minutes then slice against the grain. Serve immediately.

INGREDIENTS

- 1 Fresh Ham
- Vegetable Oil
- Big Swede BBQ Badass Beef Boost

**250°F, 121°C
45 MINS**

Grilled Pork Chops with Smoked

APPLE SAUCE

SERVES
4-6

TIME
60 MIN

METHOD
SMOKING

Smoked thick pork chops goes really well with this chunky and smoky apple sauce.

METHOD

1. Preheat your smoker or grill and set it up for smoking at 350°F or 177°C. If using wood or pellets, use apple or cherry wood.

2. Half, peel and core the apples. Place the apples cut sides down on the grates and grill for about 4 minutes or until the apples are softened and lightly blackened. Turn them over and grill for an additional 5 minutes

3. Move the apples to the upper rack of the grill. Lower the temperature to 180°F or 82°C. Let the apples absorb some smoke for about 10 minutes.

4. Transfer the apples to a cutting board and chop into one-inch chunks.
Put the chopped apples in a large saucepan and place over low heat. Add the cinnamon, allspice, salt and apple juice. Cook for about 25 minutes, covered and stirring occasionally, to form a slightly chunky applesauce. Transfer to a serving bowl and keep warm.

5. Season the pork chops with the Big Swede BBQ Badass Pork Boost or your favorite pork rub and let them sit at room temperature for 45 minutes.

6. Set the grill to 650°F or 343°C. When screaming hot, sear all the sides of the pork chops until you have nice grillmarks.

7. Lower the temperature of the grill to 250°F or 121°C and smoke the pork chops until they reach an inner temperature of 145°F or 63°C. When ready remove from the grill and let rest for 5 minutes.

8. Slice the pork chop into thin slices and serve immediately with the chunky apple sauce

250°F, 121°C
60 MINS

INGREDIENTS

- 2 Thick Pork Cops
- Big Swede BBQ Badass Pork Boost
- 5 Golden Delicious Apples
- 1 tsp Cinnamon
- 1/2 tsp Allspice
- 1/2 tsp Salt
- 2 cups Apple Juice

- Apple Juice to spritz

Smoked Crown Roast of
PORK

SERVES	TIME	METHOD
8-10	3 HRS	SMOKING

METHOD

1. Start by finely chop all the herbs and place in a bowl. Add the garlic and olive oil and whisk until it forms a paste.

2. Pat the crown pork roast dry. Season the entire roast with the Big Swede BBQ Badass Texas Boost or your favorite SPG rub. Then spread the herb paste over the entire roast.

3. Place the roast on a large plate, then tightly cover with foil or plastic wrap and refrigerate for a couple of hours but preferably overnight.

4. Remove the roast from the foil or plastic wrap. Wrap small pieces of foil over the top of each bone. This will prevent the bones from burning or charring.

5. Set your smoker or grill to 325°F or 163°C. If using wood or pellets, use fruit wood like apple or cherry.

6. Smoke until you reach an inner temperature of 150°F or 66°C, about 3 hours

7. Remove the roast from the grill and let it rest at least 20 minutes before carving. Serve table side and slice into individual chops.

**325°F, 163°C
3 HRS**

INGREDIENTS

- 1 Crown Pork Roast
- 2 Tbs Rosemary
- 2 Tbs Thyme
- 1 1/2 tbsp Sage
- 5 Garlic Cloves
- 2 Tbs olive oil
- Big Swede BBQ Badass Texas Boost

Pork Belly

BURNT ENDS

SERVES
6–8

TIME
4 HRS

METHOD
SMOKING

I just love pork belly burnt ends or pork candy. They are great as an appetizer, or throw them on some tacos or pork belly sandwiches. They melt in your mouth, and the sweet and heat combo is irresistable.

METHOD

1. Preheat your smoker or grill and set it up for smoking at 250°F or 121°C. If using wood or pellets, use apple or cherry wood.

2. Start by trimming any excess fat from the pork belly and then slice the pork belly into one-inch cubes.

3. Season the pork belly with the Big Swede BBQ Badass Pork Boost or your favorite sweet pork rub. Let the pork belly cubes sit for 45 minutes to allow the rub to adhere to the pork.

4. Place in the grill on an elevated rack with an aluminum pan underneath (pork belly is very fatty and the aluminum pan will help keep the grill clean, so you don't risk a grease fire).

5. Smoke for 3 hours. Check to ensure that the rub is set on the pork belly cubes.

6. Remove the pork belly cubes from the smoker and place in a new aluminum pan. Add half of the barbecue sauce, all the butter, brown sugar and honey. Toss until all the pork belly cubes are covered.

7. Cover with aluminum foil and cook for another hour or until the meat registers at around 203°F or 95°C.

8. Uncover the pan, toss with the remaining BBQ sauce and smoke for another 15 minutes.

9. Remove from the smoker and let rest for 10 minutes. Serve immediately.

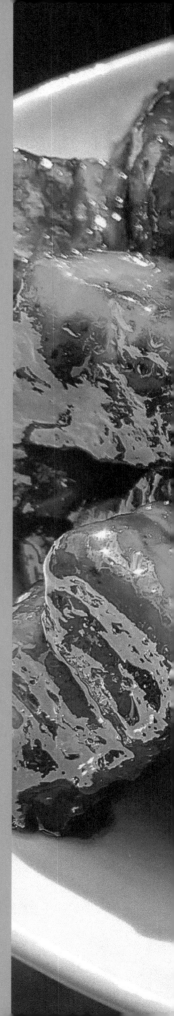

INGREDIENTS

- 5 lb Pork Belly
- Big Swede BBQ Badass Pork Boost
- 1 1/2 cup Barbecue Sauce
- 3 Tbs Butter
- 3 Tbs Honey
- 1/2 cup Brown Sugar

Smoked
ASIAN RIBS

SERVES	TIME	METHOD
4–6	5 HRS	SMOKING

Sweet sticky ribs loaded with asian flavors – they are messy but so good!

METHOD

1. Remove the membranes from the back of ribs and then trim off any excess fat.

2. Season the ribs on both sides with the Big Swede BBQ Badass Pork Boost or your favorite sweet BBQ rub. Pat the meat to ensure that the rub adhere to the meat. Let is set for 35 minutes.

3. Set your smoker or grill to 275°F or 125°C. If using wood or pellets, use cherry or apple wood.

4. Place the ribs in the grill and cook for 2 hours. Spritz with some water if the ribs get too dry. When the ribs reach a mahogany color and the bark is set, remove them from the smoker.

5. Place a sauce pan over medium heat and add honey, brown sugar, balsamic vinegar, soy sauce, garlic, ginger, and sriracha. Bring mixture to a boil, then turn down heat. Use half of this sauce for wrapping and reduce the other half by half and use for glaze.

6. Place each rib on two sheets of aluminum foil. Pour sauce over the rack. Close the foil carefully and repeat for the other slabs.

7. Place the wrapped ribs back on the grill and continue to cook for 2 hours or until tender. Be sure to check the ribs for tenderness at the 90–minute mark.

8. When a few of the larger bones are exposed on the back and the slab bends easily when lifted, the ribs are ready to come off the grill. Open the foil and let the ribs steam for a couple of minutes. Inner temperature should be around 202°F or 95°C.

9. Glace the ribs with the reduced Asian sauce and then sprinkle with sesame seeds and green onions. Slice and serve immediately.

INGREDIENTS

- 3 racks Baby Back Ribs
- Big Swede BBQ Badass Pork Boost
- 1 Tbs Sesame Seeds
- 3 Green Onions, sliced

Asian Sauce:
- 1 cup Honey
- 1 cup Brown Sugar
- 2/3 cup Mirin Rice Wine
- 1 cup Soy Sauce
- 2 Tbs Garlic, minced
- 1 Tbs Ginger Powder
- 1 Tbs Sriracha Sauce

Scalloped Ring
BOLOGNA

SERVES	TIME	METHOD
4-6	30 MINS	BAKING

METHOD

1. Start by removing the casing from the ring bologna. Make incisions in the sausage 3/4 to the bottom about one inch apart. Lightly season each bologna with the Big Swede BBQ Badass Pork Boost or your favorite pork rub.

2. Slice the apples into very thin slices and cut these in half.

3. Smear every incision with the mustard and ensure that the mustard really gets into each opening. Then insert an apple slice into each incision as well.

4. Then smear the top of each bologna with plenty of mustard as well. Next, top each bologna with the shredded cheese. Pat the top of the bologna so the cheese doesn't fall off. Place the sausages in an aluminum pan.

5. Set the grill to 425°F or 218°C. If using wood or pellets, use cherry wood.

6. Insert the pan into the smoker and bake for 30 minutes. Add more cheese if needed throughout the bake. When the cheese is melted and turning golden, remove it from the grill.

7. Serve the scalloped ring bologna with mashed potatoes.

**425°F, 218°C
30 MINS**

INGREDIENTS

- 1 lb Ring Bologna (preferable Swedish Falukorv)
- 2 Apples, peeled and cored
- 1 cup Wholegrain or German Mustard
- 1 cup Extra Sharp Cheddar, shredded
- Big Swede BBQ Badass Pork Boost

Smoked and Pulled
PORK

SERVES	TIME	METHOD
4–6	7 HRS	SMOKING

METHOD

1. Start by trimming some of the thicker and harder fatty parts of the pork butt or shoulder. Leave some fat on the meat since it has flavor.

2. Combine your favorite pork injection with apple juice according to instructions. Inject the butt with the marinade. Move throughout the butt and inject thoroughly. Refrigerate for at least 5 hours or overnight.

3. Generously sprinkle the Big Swede BBQ Badass Pork Boost or your favorite pork rub over the pork butt and let it sit for an hour – this will allow the rub to penetrate and adhere to the meat.

4. Set your smoker to 230°F or 110°C. If using wood or pellets, use cherry wood.

5. Place the butt in the grill on an elevated rack with the fat side towards the heat. Also place an aluminum pan with beef broth underneath the butt to collect all the drippings.

6. Smoke for about 5 hours or until the internal temperature reaches about 165°F or 74°C. When you have a nice bark – wrap the pork butt tightly in aluminum foil.

7. Keep smoking until the internal temperature reaches about 205°F or 96°C. While you wait for the butt to reach that temperature, collect all the drippings and pour into a tall container. Put the container in the fridge, the temperature will make the fat rise and get stiff. After an hour or so spoon out all the coagulated fat and save the concentrated pork juice.

8. The last step is to let the meat rest for at least an hour. Use food handling gloves to pull the meat apart into nice chunks. Use a fork to shred some of the pork that is falling apart. Pour back some of the dripping liquid into the shredded pork. Serve while hot.

INGREDIENTS

- 1 Pork Butt or Shoulder
- Big Swede BBQ Badass Pork Boost
- 1 cup Apple Juice
- Commercial Pork Injection
- 2 liters Beef Broth

 **230°F, 110°C
7 HRS**

Smoked Pork and Corn
SOUP

SERVES
4–6

TIME
45 MINS

METHOD
GRILLING

METHOD

1. Light or set your grill to direct hot heat, about 650°F or 345°C. If using wood or charcoal, use fruit wood like cherry, peach or apple.

2. Oil the corn with some vegetable oil and season with the Big Swede BBQ Badass Veggie Boost or your favorite herb seasoning.

3. Grill the ears of corn for 5 minutes turning every minute. When nicely charred, remove from the grill and let cool. When cooled down, slice the kernels from the ears.

4. Lower the temperature of the grill to 350°F or 177°C.

5. Pour the olive oil into a heavy cast iron pan and place in the grill.

6. Add the onions and sauté until translucent, about 5 minutes. Add the corn and stir. Stir in the cumin and the Big Swede BBQ Badass Burger Boost or your favorite umami seasoning. Cook for 1 minute, stirring constantly.

7. Add chicken broth and scrape the bottom of the pan to deglaze it.

8. Stir in the green chiles, fire roasted salsa, diced tomatoes and pulled pork. Simmer for 20–25 minutes.

9. When ready, remove from the grill and mix in the cilantro. Serve immediately.

INGREDIENTS

- 1 lb Pulled Pork, chopped
- 1 Tbs Extra Virgin Olive Oil
- 1 Onion, chopped
- 3 ears Corn, shucked
- 2 Tbs Vegetable Oil
- 1 Tbs Ground Cumin
- 1 Tbs Big Swede BBQ Badass Burger Boost
- 1 Tbs Big Swede BBQ Badass Veggie Boost
- 4 cups Chicken Broth
- 8 oz Green Chiles
- 15 oz Fire Roasted Salsa
- 15 oz Diced Tomatoes
- 1/2 cup Cilantro, chopped

INGREDIENTS

- 1 rack Iberico Pork Loin (Chuletero)
- Big Swede BBQ Badass Pork Boost
- 1 cup Orange Juice
- 3 Sweet Potatoes, peeled and diced
- 2 Tbs Butter
- 2 tsp Cinnamon
- 1/2 tsp Chipotle Powder
- 2/3 cup Agave Nectar
- 1 Tbs Coriander Seed
- Salt and Pepper, to taste

Orange Sweet Potatoes and Smoked

IBERICO LOIN

SERVES	TIME	METHOD
4–6	90 MINS	SMOKING

The Iberico Pork Loin is extremely marbled with rich and nutty flavors and thanks to the incredible quality it should never be overcooked.

METHOD

1. In a large saucepot, add the diced sweet potatoes. Cover them with water and bring to a boil. Boil the sweet potatoes until fork tender. Remove the water from the pan, add the butter and blend with an immersion blender until smooth. Add the cinnamon, chipotle, 1/3 cup of the agave and 1/2 cup of the orange juice, mix, and keep warm.

2. Set your smoker or grill to 250°F or 121°C. If using wood or pellets, use pecan or maple wood.

3. Trim some of the excess fat from the Iberico Pork Loin and season all over with the Big Swede BBQ Badass Pork Boost or your favorite sweet BBQ rub. Place the pork loin in the smoker on an elevated rack.

4. Make the orange juice baste by combining the remaining orange juice, the agave nectar and the coriander seed in a small bowl.

5. Smoke the pork loin until it reaches and inner temperature of 145°F or 63°C, about 90 minutes. Every 15 minutes baste lightly with the orange juice baste.

6. When the pork loin is ready, remove from the smoker and let rest in aluminum foil for 15 minutes.

7. Slice the loin into chops. Brush the sides with the basting liquid. Place each chop over a dollop of the orange sweet potatoes and serve immediately.

INGREDIENTS

- 2 Pork Tenderloins
- Big Swede BBQ Badass Pork Boost
- Duckfat Spray

Roasted Potatoes and Mushrooms:
- 4 Tbs Butter
- 1 Garlic Head, minced
- 2 cups Baby Potatoes, sliced
- 2 cups Chanterelle Mushrooms
- 1 cup Green Beans, sliced
- 1 Tbs Rosemary, chopped
- 1 Tbs Thyme, chopped
- 1 Tbs Big Swede BBQ Badass Veggie
  Boost
- 3 Tbs Soy Sauce

Smoked Pork
TENDERLOIN

——————●——————

SERVES	TIME	METHOD
4-6	75 MINS	SMOKING

Smoked pork and roasted potatoes makes a hearty and rustic dinner.

METHOD

1. Trim the pork tenderloins and remove silverskin and any excess fat. Season with the Big Swede BBQ Badass Pork Boost or your favorite pork seasoning. Let the pork tenderloins sit for 45 minutes to allow the seasoning to adhere.

2. Set your grill or smoker to 225°F or 107°C. If you are using wood or pellets, use cherry wood.

3. Place the pork tenderloins in the smoker and smoke until they reach an inner temperature of 135°F or 57°C, about 60 minutes. Spray with some duckfat spray when the tenderloins look dry.

4. While the tenderloins are smoking, place the potatoes in a small pot and add enough water to cover the top. Add half the soy sauce and boil the potatoes for 10 minutes or until just cooked. Remove from pan and let cool.

5. In a pan or skillet, melt butter over medium heat and

sauté garlic until tender.

6. Add the mushrooms and sauté for 3 minutes. Slice the potatoes into slices and add both potatoes and beans to the pan as well.

7. Cook the potatoes, beans and mushrooms until edges are starting to brown. Add the herbs, the Big Swede BBQ Badass Veggie Boost and the rest of the soy sauce. Cook for another minute then remove from pan.

8. When the pork tenderloin hits the inner temperature, remove from the smoker and increase the temperature to 650°F or 343°C.

9. When the grates are hot, grill the pork tenderloins for a couple of minutes to get a good caramelized surface and a nice char.

10. Remove the tenderloins from the smoker, let them rest for 5 minutes and then serve them with the potatoes.

SEA

Seafood

Fishing with my dad is one of my fondest childhood memories. Growing up, I always lived near water. And every fall we rented a small cabin by a lake for a couple of weeks, where we foraged lingonberries, blueberries and mushrooms. And we went fishing. A lot.

I can still remember my dad waking me up before the sunrise and help me put on some warm clothes. The two of us quietly walking down to the lake in anticipation. Brushing my teeth using the clear and cold lake water. Slowly pushing the small rowing boat into the water, and then putting on the life west. Always safety first. And then slowly rowing out on the completely calm lake. Finding a good fishing spot while the night is turning into dawn with the lake looking like a mirror hidden in the morning mist. Listening to the birds waking up in the background.

The anticipation and excitement: Will we catch anything?

And then the thrill of feeling the first jerk on the line. The joy when you bring the captured fish to the boat. Rinsing and cleaning the fish when you return to shore. And then slowly sautéing these fresh fish fillets with salt, pepper and tons of butter.

Yeah, I love seafood.

FOOD

Coconut and Lime
SHRIMP

SERVES
4-6

TIME
20 MINS

METHOD
GRILLING

METHOD

1. In a large bowl, whisk all marinade ingredients to combine. Add the shrimp and marinade them in the fridge for at least 4 hours, preferably overnight. Turn them a few times to make sure they are evenly marinated.

2. Bring chicken broth, coconut milk and salt to a boil in a large saucepan. Stir in rice. Cover the pan and reduce the heat. Simmer for 15 minutes or until liquid is absorbed and rice is tender.

3. Remove from heat and let the rice sit for 5 minutes. Then toss the rice gently with the mangoes and the pistachios.

4. Brush the grill lightly with vegetable oil and set the temperature to 500°F or 260°C. If using wood or pellets, use peach or apple.

5. Thread shrimp onto skewers, piercing each shrimp near the head and tail.

6. Cook for 2-3 minutes per side until shrimp turn pink. When ready, remove the skewers from the grill.

7. Remove the shrimp from the skewers and serve on top of the Caribbean rice. Garnish with chopped cilantro.

**500°F, 260°C
6 MINS**

INGREDIENTS

- 1 lb Shrimp peeled, deveined, and tails removed
- Cilantro, for garnish
- Vegetable Oil

Shrimp Marinade:
- 2 Limes, zested and juiced
- 1/2 cup Coconut Milk
- 1/4 cup Pineapple Juice
- 2 Tbs Soy Sauce
- 1 Tbs Brown Sugar
- 2 Tbs Hot Sauce
- 2 Tbs Garlic, minced
- 1 Tbs Extra Virgin Olive Oil

Caribbean Rice:
- 1 1/3 cups Chicken Broth
- 14 oz Coconut Milk
- 1 tsp Salt
- 2 cups Jasmine Rice
- 1 cup Mango, diced
- 1/2 cup Pistachios, chopped roasted and salted

INGREDIENTS

- 2 Salmon Fillets
- 2 Tbs Extra Virgin Olive Oil
- Big Swede BBQ Badass Seafood Boost
- 1 stick Butter, unsalted
- 1 Lemon, sliced

Smoked
SALMON FILLETS

SERVES	TIME	METHOD
4-6	60 MINS	SMOKING

This smoked salmon recipe turns an ordinary piece of fish into an extraordinary, melt-in-your-mouth, flavorful morsel that will become a new favorite with just your first bite.

METHOD

1. Pull any pin bones out from the salmon fillets with tweezers. Flip the fish over so the flesh side is down. Use the non-sharpened side of a fillet knife or a boning knife to remove the scales by running it along the skin against the grain of the scales pattern. Rinse the salmon fillets and pat dry.

2. Brush the salmon fillets with a thin layer of olive oil then season gently with the Big Swede BBQ Badass Seafood Boost or your favorite seafood herb rub. Let sit for 30 minutes. Slice the butter into thin slices.

3. Set your smoker or grill to 250°F or 121°C. If using wood or pellets, use pecan or maple wood.

4. Place the cast iron pan with the seasoned salmon fillets in the center of your grill. Place 2/3 of the butter slices on top of the salmon fillets. Smoke the salmon until it reaches an internal temperature of 145°F or 63°C, approximately 50–60 minutes.

5. When the butter is melted, approximately 10-15 minutes into the cook, slice the lemon into thin slices and place on the salmon. Add the remaining slices of butter on top of the lemon slices.

6. Remove the cast iron pan from the grill and let the salmon rest for 3-4 minutes. Carefully remove the fillets from the cast iron pan. The skin might stick but that is ok – we don't need it in this recipe. Serve

INGREDIENTS

- 12 Large Oysters
- 8 Tbs Butter
- 1 Tbs Big Swede BBQ Badass Seafood Boost
- 1/4 cup Basil Leaves
- 1/2 cup Parmesan Cheese, grated
- 1 Tbs Lemon Juice
- 1/2 Lemon, zested
- 2 Garlic Cloves, minced

Grilled
OYSTERS

SERVES	TIME	METHOD
4-6	4 MINS	GRILLING

METHOD

1. Set your smoker or grill to 600°F or 315°C. If using wood or pellets, use pecan or maple wood.

2. Let the butter sit in room temperature until soften. Add the Big Swede BBQ Badass Seafood Boost or your favorite seafood herb seasoning, the basil, the parmesan cheese, the lemon juice and zest and the garlic to the butter. Mix thoroughly and set aside.

3. Line a rimmed baking sheet with heavy-duty aluminum foil, crinkling it up to create deep creases.

4. Shuck oysters, discard top shells, and place them on foil-lined baking sheet, using the foil to keep them upright so that oyster juices do not spill out.

5. Using 2 spoons, place a tablespoon of compound butter on top of each oyster and place the baking sheet in the grill.

6. Cover and cook until butter is melted, and liquid is bubbling, about 3 minutes. When ready, remove from the grill

7. Pour some coarse sea salt into a serving tray and place the oyster in the salt. This will help to keep the oysters upright and straight when serving, so the liquid inside won't spill. Serve immediately.

Traditional Seafood
PAELLA

SERVES	TIME	METHOD
2-3	30 MINS	GRILLING

INGREDIENTS

- 2 Tbs Extra Virgin Olive Oil
- 3 Garlic Cloves, minced
- 1 Onion, finely diced
- 1 Red Pepper, finely diced
- 1 Tomato, peeled and diced
- 1 1/2 cups Paella Rice
- 6 cups Seafood Broth
- 1 tsp Saffron Threads
- 1 Tbs Big Swede BBQ Badass Seafood Boost
- 8 Argentine Red Shrimp, deveined
- 10 large Black Mussels
- 10 Little Neck Clams

400°F, 204°C
10 MINS

METHOD

1. Heat up the seafood broth in a saucepan and add the saffron threads. Simmer for 5 minutes and then set aside.

2. Light or set your grill to direct medium heat, about 400°F or 204°C. If using wood or charcoal, use pecan or maple wood.

3. Heat up a paella pan or large skillet in the grill.

4. Add and heat up the olive oil in the skillet and add the onion and cook for three minutes until translucent.

5. Add garlic and cook for another minute. Then add red pepper and cook until softened. Next, add tomato and cook for 1 minute to soften.

6. Add the paella rice and mix until all the grains are coated in in the vegetable mix.

7. Add the seafood broth with saffron, stir once, then leave until it starts simmering. Season with the Big Swede BBQ Badass Seafood Boost or your favorite seafood seasoning. Cook for another 7-8 minutes. It is ok to stir during this phase.

8. Place the prawns into the rice, squidging it in so they are mostly immersed, then push the mussels and clams in so they are partially immersed as well. Cook for 10 - 15 minutes or until prawns are opaque, mussels are open and most of the liquid has evaporated. Discard any mussels or clams that do not open.

9. Do not stir the paella during this phase – this will allow a beautiful crust to form at the bottom which is the signature of any good paella – the Socarrat.
Rest for 5 minutes before serving.

INGREDIENTS

- 1 Sea Bass
- 3 lbs Kosher Salt
- 8 Juniper Berries
- 8 Black Peppercorn
- 2 Egg Whites
- 5 Thyme Sprigs
- 1 Lemon
- Big Swede BBQ Badass
  Seafood Boost
- Water

Salt Baked
SEABASS

SERVES	TIME	METHOD
2–3	30 MINS	BAKING

This is the most bulletproof way to cook whole fish on a grill – it will turn out perfect every single time

METHOD

1. Set your grill or smoker to 450°F or 232°C.

2. Rinse the sea bass thoroughly (you can also use branzino, trout or snappers for this recipe). Slice the lemon and season the lemon slices on both sides with the Big Swede BBQ Badass Seafood Boost or your favorite seafood herb seasoning. Stuff the sea bass with lemon slices and thymes sprigs.

3. Line a rimmed baking sheet with a piece of foil. Combine salt, egg whites, juniper berries and black peppercorns in a bowl. Add water gradually and mix until the mix has the consistency of wet sand.

4. Spread half the salt mixture on the prepared baking sheet in a rectangle just larger than the fish.

5. Place the stuffed sea bass on the salt and pat the remaining salt mixture over the fish to cover completely.

6. Place the baking sheet with the salt covered sea bass in the grill.

7. Bake the sea bass in the grill for about 30 minutes. It is ready when the salt crust is hard and starting to get a light brown color.

8. Remove from the grill and let cool for 2 minutes.

9. Using a large spoon, tap all around the edge of the salt crust to loosen it. Remove the salt top and carefully remove the skin. Wipe away any stray salt.

10. Use an offset spatula to remove the top fillet from the bones and transfer to a warmed serving plate. Remove the bones and lift away the bottom fillet and place it on the plate as well.

11. Gently scrape off the herbs and lemon slices. Plate the fish fillets and squeeze a little lemon juice over the fish. Serve immediately.

INGREDIENTS

- 6 Lobster Tails
- Duckfat Spray
- Big Swede BBQ Badass Seafood Boost
- 1 Tbs Butter, unsalted
- 1 lb Mushrooms, quartered
- 1 Onion, finely chopped
- 1 Tbs Flour
- 1 1/2 cup Heavy Cream
- 1/2 cup Seafood Stock, concentrated
- 1 Tbs Cognac
- 1 Tbs Dijon Mustard
- 1/2 tsp Cayenne Pepper
- Salt and Pepper
- 1 bunch Dill, finely chopped
- 1 cup Parmesan Cheese, grated
- Lemon Slices for garnish
- Dill Sprigs, for garnish

Lobster
AU GRATIN

SERVES	TIME	METHOD
4-6	25 MINUTES	GRILLING

The rich lobster flavors in this luxurious and creamy gratin will make it an instant hit at your BBQ

METHOD

1. Set up your grill or smoker to 550°F or 288°C. If using wood or pellets, use pecan or maple wood.

2. Cut the lobster tails in half and spray the meat side with duckfat spray. Season the lobster tails with the Big Swede BBQ Badass Seafood Boost or your favorite seafood herb seasoning.

3. Grill the lobster tails for 2 minutes, meat side down. Flip them over and grill for another 90 seconds. Remove from the grill and let cool.

4. When cooled down, remove the lobster meat from the lobster tails and chop into small chunks. Save both the tails and meat for later.

5. Place a heavy cast iron skillet in the grill and heat it up for 3 minutes. Melt the butter and then add the mushrooms and the onion. Cook until lightly brown about 5 minutes.

6. Add the flour and the heavy cream and let it cook for one minute while stirring. The mixture should thicken up slightly. Add the concentrated seafood stock, cognac, Dijon mustard, and cayenne pepper. Continue to cook for 3 minutes and then season with salt and pepper.

7. Add the finely chopped dill and the lobster meat to the pan. Mix carefully.

8. Lower the temperature on the grill or smoker to 425°F or 218°C.

9. Place the lobster shells in a cast iron pan and then fill them with the lobster mix. Pour the rest of the mix over the filled shells. Sprinkle the parmesan cheese on top.

10. Bake the gratin in the grill or smoker for 10 minutes or until the cheese is melting and bubbling.

11. Serve by plating the filled lobster shells.

12. Garnish with lemon and dill and serve immediately.

INGREDIENTS

- 2 Striped Bass, cleaned and scaled
- 2 Tbs Extra Virgin Olive Oil
- 1 bunch Parsley
- 2 Lemons
- 5 Garlic Cloves, crushed
- Salt and Pepper

New Potatoes with Dill:
- 2 lbs New Potatoes, boiled
- Salt and Pepper, to taste
- 2 Tbs Butter, unsalted
- 2 Tbs Extra Virgin Olive Oil
- 1 Lemon, juiced
- 3 Tbs Dill, chopped plus sprigs for garnish

Chives Dressing:
- 2 cups Crème Fraiche
- 2 Garlic Cloves, mashed
- 2 Tbs Yellow Onion, finely chopped
- 3 Tbs Chives, finely chopped
- Chives, cut into 2 inch stalks
- Salt and pepper, to taste

Grilled Striped
BASS

SERVES | **TIME** | **METHOD**
4-6 | 12 MINS | GRILLING

Nothing is better on warm summer evenings than opening up a chilled bottle of chardonnay and eat freshly grilled fish with new potatoes and a light dressing

METHOD

1. Start preparing the chives dressing and mix all the ingredients for the dressing in a large bowl. Season with salt and pepper. Put in the refrigerator to keep cool. Just before serving, top the dressing with additional stalks of chives.

2. Set your grill or smoker to 600°F or 315°C. If you are using wood or pellets, use maple wood.

3. Pat the fish dry with paper towels and then carefully score the skin of the fish on both sides. Be careful not to cut into the meat. Brush the fish all over with olive oil and season generously inside and out with salt and pepper. Stuff the cavity with the parsley, garlic, and the lemon slices.

4. Brush the grates with oil. Grill the fish over moderately high heat, uncovered, until lightly charred and it releases easily from the grill grates, about 5-6 minutes. Turn and grill until the flesh is white throughout, 5-6 minutes longer.

5. At the same time, combine the butter and olive oil in a large cast iron pan. Place the pan on the grill as well and heat until the butter melts and starts to sizzle. Add the boiled new potatoes and cook, stirring occasionally, until the potatoes are browned and starting to crisp, about 12 minutes.

6. Remove the pan from the grill and season the new potatoes with salt and sprinkle with the lemon juice and chopped dill. Set aside.

7. Transfer the fish to a platter and let rest for 5 minutes. Drizzle with oil and serve the fish with the new potatoes and the chives dressing.

Toast
SKAGEN

SERVES	TIME	METHOD
4-6	5 MINS	GRILLING

INGREDIENTS

- 1 1/2 lbs North Atlantic Shrimp
- 1 cup Mayonnaise
- 1 cup Crème Fraiche
- 2 Red Onions, finely chopped
- 1 tsp Horseradish
- 2 tsp Brandy
- 4 oz Dijon Mustard
- 4 oz Whitefish Roe
- Salt and White Pepper
- 5 Tbs Dill, finely chopped
- 6 Slices of Sourdough Bread
- 2 Tbsp Duckfat spray
- 1 bunch Dill Sprigs, for garnish
- Caviar for garnish

650°F, 343°C
5 MINS

I love Toast Skagen so much that I grilled the sourdough bread to be able to include the recipe in this book

METHOD

1. Set up your grill for direct grilling high heat, 650°F or 343°C. If using wood or pellets, use fruit wood.

2. Mix the mayonnaise, crème fraiche, and Dijon mustard together. Add salt and freshly ground white pepper to taste. You can also add some brandy or some horseradish if you want to. Add the whitefish roe and stir.

3. Clean the shrimp and add to the mayo mix. Finely chop the dill and add as well. Stir and keep chilled.

4. Spray the sourdough bread slices with the duckfat on both sides. Grill until nicely charred with beautiful sear marks. For a better presentation, cut off the edges and cut bread in half diagonally.

5. When ready to serve, pile the shrimp mix on top of the grilled bread and garnish with a dollop of caviar, a sprig of dill and a lemon wedge. You can also garnish with some chives or green onions. The Toast Skagen is best served on warm bread and cold shrimp mix so serve immediately.

Grilled Moules
MARINIERE

SERVES	TIME	METHOD
2-4	10 MINS	GRILLING

INGREDIENTS

- 2 lbs Black Mussels
- 3 Tbs Butter
- 1 Leek, finely chopped
- 1/2 Yellow Onion, finely chopped
- 2 Tbs Garlic, minced
- 1 cup Chardonnay
- 2 Tbs Big Swede BBQ Badass Seafood Boost
- 2 Tbs Parsley, finely chopped
- 1/2 cup Heavy Cream

400°F, 204°C
10 MINS

METHOD

1. Light or set your grill to direct medium heat, about 400°F or 204°C. If using wood or charcoal, use pecan or maple wood.

2. Rinse and clean the mussels thoroughly. Remove any mussels that are already open.

3. Place a heavy cast iron pan on the grill and add half of the butter.

4. When the butter is melted, add the leek, onion and garlic to the butter and sauté for 2 minutes or until translucent.

5. Add the wine and reduce to half, about 3 minutes.

6. Add the mussels and cover the pan. Cook for 2-3 minutes or until the mussels are opened. Remove any mussels that are still closed.

7. Remove the cast iron pan from the grill. Add the remaining butter and stir. Add the parsley and the Big Swede BBQ Badass Seafood Boost or your favorite seafood rub and stir.

8. Add the heavy cream and serve immediately.

Grilled Salmon
FLATBREAD

SERVES
4-6

TIME
6 MINS

METHOD
BAKING

INGREDIENTS

- 4 Flatbreads
- 2 Tbs Garlic-infused Olive Oil
- 2 cups Boursin Garlic and Herb Cheese
- 1/2 lb Smoked Salmon
- Big Swede BBQ Badass Seafood Boost
- 2 cups Baby Arugula
- 1 Lemon, zested
- 1 bunch Dill Sprigs, to garnish
- Balsamic Glaze

METHOD

1. Set your grill or smoker to 400°F or 204°C. If using wood or pellets, use pecan or maple wood.

2. Brush the flatbreads on one side with a thin layer of the garlic-infused olive oil.

3. Crumble plenty of the Boursin cheese on top of the flatbreads and then season lightly with the Big Swede BBQ Badass Seafood Boost or your favorite seafood herb seasoning.

4. Tear the smoked salmon into smaller pieces and scatter on top of the flatbreads.

5. Place the flatbreads in the grill or smoker and bake until the cheese is melting, and the flatbreads are getting a nice golden bottom crust, between 4-6 minutes. Remove from the grill.

6. Scatter the baby arugula leaves on top of the baked flatbreads and then zest the lemon on top of the leaves.

7. Tear the dill leaves of the sprigs and place plenty of dill on top of the flatbreads.

8. Last but not least, drizzle the flatbreads with the balsamic glaze and then serve immediately.

Juniper Smoked
SALMON

SERVES
4–6

TIME
10 MINS

METHOD
GRILLING

METHOD

1. Mix the salt, sugar and the Big Swede BBQ Seafood Boost into a dry brine. Smear the salmon with this mix and let it sit in the fridge for 48 hrs. Turn the salmon every 12 hours.

2. Soak fresh juniper branches in water for at least 1 hr.

3. Mix sour cream, chives and horseradish cream in a bowl and set aside.

4. Set your grill or smoker to 500°F or 260°C. If using wood or pellets, use peach or apple.

5. Remove the salmon from the fridge and pat dry with a paper towel. Let it sit for 20 minutes in room temperature.

6. Place the soaked juniper branches on top of the fire in the grill. Then place the salmon fillets on top of the juniper branches. Let it smoke for 8–10 minutes. If the juniper branches light on fire, spray them with some water from a spray bottle. Squeeze some lemon juice on top of the salmon and remove from the grill.

7. Serve immediately with the Horseradish Sour Cream and Wasa Crisp Bread.

INGREDIENTS

- 2 Tbs Salt
- 1 Tbs Sugar
- 1 Tbs Big Swede BBQ Badass Seafood Boost
- 1 cup Sour Creme
- 2 Tbs Chives, chopped
- 1 Tbs Horseradish Cream
- 1 Lemon
- Wasa Swedish Crisp Bread

500°F or 260°C.
45 MINS

Shrimp and Corn

MAQUE CHOUX

SERVES
4–6

TIME
30 MINS

METHOD
GRILLING

Grilling these large Red Argentine Shrimp in their shells
protects the delicate meat and infuses them with smoky flavors

INGREDIENTS

- 2 lbs Red Argentine Shrimp
- 3/4 cup Extra Virgin Olive Oil
- 5 Tbs Garlic, minced
- 2 Tbs Creole Seasoning
- 2 Tbs Big Swede BBQ Badass Seafood Boost
- 4 Ears of Corn
- 3 Tbs Butter
- 1 Red Onion, finely chopped
- 2 Bell Peppers, finely chopped
- 4 stalks Celery, finely chopped
- 1 Poblano Pepper, finely choped
- 6 Green Onions, finely chopped, white and green parts seperated
- 3 Thyme Sprigs
- 1/3 cup Vermouth
- 3/4 cup Shrimp Broth, concentrated
- 1/2 cup Heavy Cream
- 2 Tbs Brandy or Cognac
- Salt and Pepper, to taste

METHOD

1. Mix the olive oil with the garlic, creole seasoning and the Big Swede BBQ Badass Seafood Boost or your favorite seafood rub. Clean and devein the shrimp but leave the shell on. Mix the cleaned shrimp with the marinade. Set aside in the fridge for at least 4 hours.

2. Set up your grill for direct grilling high heat, 650°F or 343°C. If using wood or pellets, use pecan or maple wood.

3. Oil the ears of corn and grill for 10-12 minutes until charred and cooked through. Set aside to cool.

4. Place a heavy cast iron pan on the grill and melt the butter. Then add the onion, bell pepper, celery, poblano and the white part of the green onions. Sauté over high heat for 5 minutes.

5. Cut the kernels of the corn stalks and add to the pan. Also add the thyme and sauté for 2 more minutes.

6. Deglaze the pan with the vermouth and scrape the bottom of the pan with a wooden spoon to release all the scrapings. Add the broth and the cream and cook for two more minutes and then keep warm.

7. Remove the shrimp from the marinade and skewer on wooden skewers. Place the skewered shrimp on the grill and grill for 3 minutes. Flip them over and continue grilling for another two minutes or until they have an inner temperature of 145°F or 63°C. Flambé with the brandy and remove from the grill.

8. Remove the shrimp from the skewers and place on top of the Maque Choux. Sprinkle with the green parts of the green onions and serve immediately.

650°F, 345°C
30 MINS

Smoked Shrimp and Avocado
BAGUETTE

SERVES
2-4

TIME
45 MINS

METHOD
SMOKING

INGREDIENTS

- 1 lbs North Atlantic Shrimp, cooked and frozen
- 2 Avocados
- 1 Lemon
- 1 bunch Dill Sprigs
- 2 French Baquettes

Garlic Aioli:
- 2 Egg Yolks
- 1 1/2 tsp Lemon juice
- 1 Garlic Clove, finely minced
- 1 tsp Dijon Mustard
- 1 1/2 cup Extra Virgin Olive Oil
- Salt, to taste
- Lemon Juice, to taste

METHOD

1. Mix together the egg yolk, lemon juice, garlic, and mustard in a bowl until combined and slightly frothy. Next, add in about 1/2 to 1 tsp of olive oil slowly while continuing to mix completely incorporated. Then, slowly pour in the olive oil while continuing to vigorously whisk until all of the oil has been added and the aioli has been emulsified and is thick. Finish by adding in lemon juice and salt. Set aside in fridge.

2. Set your grill or smoker to 150°F or 65°C, or your lowest setting. If using wood or pellets, use maple or pecan wood.

3. Place the frozen shrimp in a seafood basket and place in the smoker. You can use both peeled or unpeeled North Atlantic Shrimp for this recipe. They must be completely frozen.

4. Smoke the shrimp for

between 30–40 minutes or until they are getting warm to the touch. They are already cooked and we don't want to overcook them. If using fresh shrimp, keep smoking until they are cooked through. Then remove from the smoker.

5. If using unpeeled shrimp, peel them by twisting their head off, and then removing the midsection and pulling off the tail.

6. Slice the baguette in half and smear the inside with the garlic aioli. By closing and then opening the baguette you get a nice spread. Slice the avocado into thin slices and place in the baguette. Next add plenty of smoked shrimp.

7. Lastly, place fresh dill on the shrimp baguette and squeeze some lemon juice on top. Also garnish with some lemon slices. Serve immediately.

Soba Noodles and
SALMON

SERVES | **TIME** | **METHOD**
4-6 | **10 MINS** | **GRILLING**

METHOD

1. In a small bowl, whisk together miso, soy sauce, honey, rice vinegar, sake, green onions, ginger and sesame oil. Pour the marinade over the salmon fillets and turn to coat. Cover and marinate in the refrigerator for at least an hour. Before grilling, remove fillets from marinade and discard the marinade. Generously brush some olive oil on both sides of fish fillets.

2. Bring water to a boil. Cook the soba noodles according to the package instructions. Drain into a colander and rinse the soba noodles in a bowl of water. Drain again and transfer to a large bowl. Mix all the ingredients for the soba noodles salad marinade in a bowl and mix well. Toss everything together.

3. Set your grill or smoker to 550°F or 288°C. If using wood or pellets, use pecan or maple wood. When the grill is hot, brush the grill grates with oil.

4. Place salmon fillets on grill, skinless side down first, so that they get nice grill marks on the hot grill while the fish is still firm. Close the grill lid. Cook 1 to 3 minutes on the first side, depending on how thick the fillets are.

5. Using tongs and a metal spatula to help if necessary, carefully flip the salmon fillets onto the other side, so that the skin side is now on the grill grates. Grill for another 2-4 minutes depending on the thickness of the fillets – the salmon should be opaque when ready. Remove the fillets from and serve with the Soba Noodle Salad. Garnish with the parsley leaves.

550°F, 288°C
10 MINS

INGREDIENTS

- 6 Salmon Fillets, skin on
- 1/4 cup White Miso
- 1/3 cup Soy Sauce
- 1/4 cup Honey
- 4 Tbs Mirin Rice Wine
- 1 Tbs Toasted Sesame Oil
- 3 Green Onions, sliced
- 2 Tbs Fresh Ginger, grated
- 2 Tbs Toasted Sesame Seeds
- 2 Tbs Extra Virgin Olive Oil
- 1 Tbs Parsley Leaves, to garnish

Soba Noodle Salad:
- 8 oz Dried Soba noodles
- 2 Green Onions
- 1/2 cup Cilantro
- 1 Tbs Toasted Sesame Seeds
- 1 Tbs Vegetable Oil
- 2 Tbs Toasted Sesame Oil
- 1/2 tsp Red Pepper Flakes
- 3 Tbs Agave Nectar
- 3 Tbs Soy Sauce

INGREDIENTS

- 4 Lobster tails
- 1/2 lb Bacon, finely chopped
- 1 lb Large Elbow Macaroni

Cheese sauce:
- 24 oz Heavy Cream
- 3 Tbs White Wine
- 10 oz Gryuere Cheese, shredded
- 10 oz Aged Cheddar, shredded
- 8 oz Cream Cheese

Mac and Cheese Topping
- 1 cup Panko Bread Crumbs
- 1 cup Pecorino Cheese, shredded

MAC AND CHEESE

SERVES
3-4

TIME
100 MINS

METHOD
SMOKING

Grilled lobster tail and bacon elevates this delicious Mac and Cheese to the next level.

METHOD

1. Set your grill or smoker to 500°F or 260°C. If using wood or pellets, use maple or pecan.

2. Insert a heavy cast iron pan in the grill and heat up. When hot, add the bacon and cook until crispy, about 10-15 minutes. Remove the bacon from the pan and set aside.

3. Remove the meat from the lobster tails and cut into small chunks. Add the chunks to the cast iron pan and cook in the bacon grease until the lobster meat is turning white, about 6-8 minutes. Remove from the grill and set aside.

4. Heat up a large pan of water and add the elbow macaroni. Slowly boil until right before al dente, about 8 minutes. Drain the macaroni and set aside.

5. Pour the heavy cream and the white wine in a large sauce pan over medium heat.

Add the three cheeses and let these slowly melt while stirring constantly. When ready, set aside.

6. Mix the macaroni and the cheese sauce in a big bowl and stir. Add the bacon and the lobster and stir again making sure it is well blended. Pour the mac and cheese into a heavy cast iron pan.

7. Mix together the panko breadcrumbs and the pecorino cheese and sprinkle over the Mac and Cheese.

8. Lower the temperature in the grill to 350°F or 177°C. Insert the cast iron pan with the Mac and Cheese and bake for 45 minutes or until the topping is getting a wonderful golden color.

9. When ready, remove the lobster and bacon Mac and Cheese from the grill and serve immediately.

Game

My dad cooks a mean Moose Roast. It is one of those dishes that I always want to eat when I visit my parents in Sweden. It is not a complicated dish to make. But there is something about game meat that is very appealing to me. And growing up in Sweden, we always had access to great game meat like moose, elk, venison, deer, bear, and wild boar.

I have also included some lamb recipes in this section, mostly because a lot of people think that lamb has a gamey flavor to it.

So, what is the secret to cooking game meat?

The most important aspect of cooking great game meat is hunting, sourcing, or buying great quality game meat. An old deer tastes quite differently than a youngling. The second aspect is picking the appropriate cooking method for the cut of game you are cooking. Hot and fast or low and slow is dependent on what you are cooking. The third aspect is to use seasonings and marinades that compliments the meat and lastly, never ever overcook game meat. I'll say it again, do not overcook game meat. Most of it is very lean and will get tough if you overcook it. I like mine rare.

If you follow these guidelines and the recipes in this book, you will definitely be ahead of the game.

GAME

INGREDIENTS

- 1 lb Elk Medallions
- 1 Tbs Thyme, chopped
- 1 Tbs Rosemary, chopped
- 2 Tbs Big Swede BBQ
  Badass Texas Boost

Juniper Sauce:
- 2 Tbs Butter
- 3 Tbs Flour
- 4 cups Beef Stock
- 1 tsp Tomato Paste
- 2 Tbs Dry Sherry
- 6 Juniper Berries
- 6 Black Peppercorns
- 2 sprigs Thyme
- 1/2 cup Heavy Cream
- 1 Tbs Red Currant Jelly
- Salt, to taste

Elk Medallions in
JUNIPER SAUCE

SERVES
3-4

TIME
15 MINS

METHOD
GRILLING

Juniper berries makes a wonderful sauce for any game meats – and I especially love it with grilled elk medallions

METHOD

1. Trim silverskin and excess fat from the elk medallions.

2. In a bowl, mix the thyme, rosemary and the Big Swede BBQ Badass Texas Boost or your favorite SPG rub.

3. Season the elk medallions on both sides with the spice mix and let it rest in room temperature for 45 minutes to allow the seasoning to adhere.

4. Smash the juniper berries and the black peppercorn together in a pestle and mortar until it resembles coarse ground pepper and set aside for later.

5. Melt butter in a frying pan over medium-low heat. Stir in the flour and mix together. Cook the roux for about 5 minutes until golden while stirring constantly. When golden, add the sherry and mix.

6. Slowly whisk in the stock. Add tomato paste, thyme, juniper

berry and black pepper mixture. Turn up the heat to medium-high and cook until it thickens, about 6 more minutes.

7. Add the red currant jelly and the heavy cream and cook for another 2 minutes. Season with salt to taste and then keep warm.

8. Light or set your grill to direct grilling 600°F or 315°C. If using wood or pellets, use oak wood.

9. Grill the elk medallions for 2-3 minutes on each side until they reach an internal temperature of 125°F or 52°C. Do not overcook the elk medallions.

10. Remove the elk medallions from the grill and let them rest for 10 minutes.

11. When rested, slice them into thin slices against the grains and serve immediately with the juniper sauce.

METHOD

1. Combine egg, breadcrumbs, and milk in a small bowl and let sit for 10 minutes.

2. In a large mixing bowl, gently combine ground lamb with the onions, breadcrumb mixture, mint, lemon zest, sun dried tomatoes and spices until fully combined.

3. Form the mixture into a loaf and place on top of a heat safe silicon mat.

4. Preheat your smoker to 350°F or 177°C or set up your grill for indirect grilling. If using a grill, insert a smokebox with some soaked wood chunks for added smoke flavor.

5. Place the silicon mat with the lamb loaf into the smoker or grill and smoke for 35 minutes or until you get an inner temperature of about 130°F or 54°C.

6. Remove the meatloaf from grill and raise temperature

to 450°F or 232°C. Once temperature is reached, spray the meatloaf with duck fat and continue to cook until the internal temperature reaches 160°F or 71°C – another 10 minutes or so.

7. While the meatloaf is cooking, prepare the spiced yoghurt and the cucumber and tomato Salad.

8. Combine all ingredients for the spiced yoghurt in a small mixing bowl and season with Kosher salt. Let sit for 30 minutes to allow flavors to meld.

9. Combine all ingredients for the salad in a small mixing bowl and season with kosher salt and freshly ground black pepper.

10. When ready, remove meatloaf from smoker and rest for 5 minutes

11. Slice the lamb meatloaf and serve immediately with the spiced yogurt and the cucumber and tomato salad.

INGREDIENTS

- 2 lbs Ground Lamb
- 1/4 cup Breadcrumbs
- 2 Tbs Whole Milk
- 1 Tbs Extra Virgin Olive Oil
- 1 Onion, finely chopped and sautéed
- 4 cloves Garlic, minced
- 1 Egg
- 1/4 cup Mint, finely chopped
- 1 Lemon, zested
- 3 Tbs Sundried Tomatoes, finely chopped
- 2 tsp Ground Cilantro
- 2 tsp Ground Cumin
- 2 tsp Ground Oregano
- 2 tsp Kosher Salt
- 1 tsp Cayenne Pepper
- 1 Tbs Big Swede BBQ Badass Burger Boost
- Duckfat Spray

Spiced Yoghurt:
- 1 1/2 cups Greek Yogurt
- 1 Tbs Lemon Juice
- 2 Tbs Mint, finely chopped
- 1/2 tsp Ground Cumin
- 1/2 tsp Ground Cilantro
- 1 tsp Garlic Powder
- Kosher salt, to taste

Cucumber and Tomato Salad:
- 1 Cucumber, peeled, deseeded, and diced
- 2 Plum Tomatoes, peeled, deseeded, and finely diced
- 1 Tbs Extra Virgin Olive Oil
- 1 Tbs Lemon Juice
- 2 Tbs Parsley, finely chopped
- 1 Tbs Big Swede BBQ Badass Veggie Boost
- Salt and Pepper, to taste

Smoked Lamb

MEATLOAF

SERVES
4-6

TIME
60 MINS

METHOD
SMOKING

The rich flavors of smoked lamb meatloaf is combined with the freshness of a Cucumber and Tomato Salad and the creaminess of Spiced Yoghurt

INGREDIENTS

- 1 Venison Tenderloin
- Big Swede BBQ Badass Texas Boost
- 2 cups Pistachios, crushed
- 2 Tbs Butter

Cauliflower Purée:
- 2 Tbs Butter, unsalted
- 1 Yellow Onion, thinly sliced
- 1 Cauliflower, trimmed and cut into florets
- 1 1/2 cup Heavy Whipping Cream
- 1/2 cup Chicken Stock
- 2 sprigs Thyme
- Kosher Salt

Port Wine Reduction Sauce:
- 3 Tbs Butter, unsalted
- 1/4 cup Shallots, finely chopped
- 3/4 cup Port wine
- 1/4 cup Red wine
- 1 cup Demi Glace or Concentrated Beef Stock
- Salt and Pepper, to taste
- 1/4 cup Heavy Cream

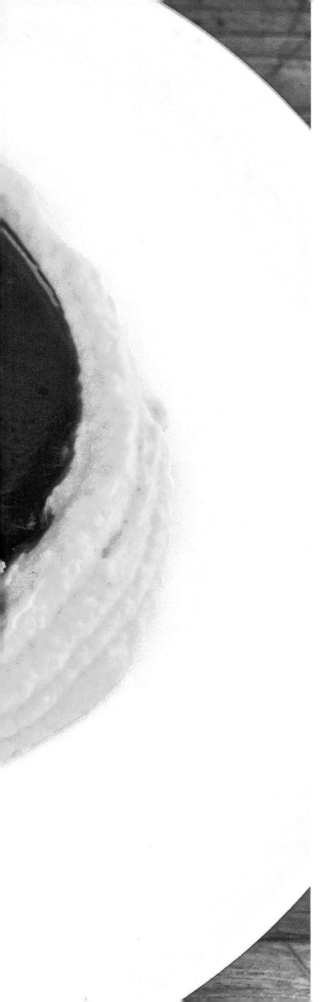

Pistachio crusted

VENISON

SERVES **TIME** **METHOD**
4-6 **12 MINS** **GRILLING**

I would be happy to eat this dish in any fine dining restaurant - the flavors are just that good

METHOD

1. Start with the port wine reduction sauce by melting the butter in a saucepan and sauté the shallots briefly until translucent. Deglaze with the port and the red wine and reduce until most of the wine has cooked off. Add the demi-glace, salt and pepper, and then simmer for approximately 5-6 minutes. Strain the sauce and add the heavy cream. Keep warm.

2. Now prepare the cauliflower purée. In a large saucepan, melt butter over medium-high heat. Add onion and cook, stirring often, until softened and translucent, about 5 minutes. Lower the heat as necessary to prevent browning.

3. Add the cauliflower, heavy cream, chicken stock, and thyme. Cover the pan, bring to a simmer, and cook, until cauliflower is tender, 5 to 6 minutes. Uncover and continue to simmer, until liquid is reduced by three-quarters, about 15-20 minutes. Discard the thyme sprig.

4. Using a blender or immersion blender, blend cauliflower and liquid on high to form a very smooth purée. Season with salt. Set aside and keep warm.

5. Set up your grill or smoker to 250°F or 121°C. If using wood or pellets, use oak wood.

6. Season the venison tenderloin with the Big Swede BBQ Badass Texas Boost or your favorite SPG rub. Heat up a skillet with the butter and quickly sear the venison tenderloin on all sides. When browned, remove and place in grill. Smoke the venison until it reaches an inner temperature of 125°F or 52°C. When ready, remove from grill and let it rest for 5 minutes in aluminum foil.

7. Pour the crushed pistachios into an aluminum pan. Roll the venison tenderloins in pistachios, making sure that the whole tenderloin is covered with pistachios. Slice and serve with the cauliflower purée and the port wine reduction sauce.

Roasted
LEG OF LAMB

SERVES
4–6

TIME
15 MINS

METHOD
SMOKING

INGREDIENTS

- 1 Leg of Lamb, boneless
- 2 Tbs Sage
- 2 Tbs Rosemary
- 2 Tbs Thyme
- 1/4 cup Lemon Juice
- 1/4 cup Dijon Mustard
- 1/3 cup Extra Virgin Olive Oil
- 4 cloves Garlic, minced
- Big Swede BBQ Badass Texas Boost
- 1 stick Butter, unsalted

METHOD

1. Finely chop the sage, rosemary and thyme leaves. Mix the herbs with lemon juice, mustard, garlic and olive oil. Whisk until you have a coarse paste.

2. Season the boneless leg of lamb with the Big Swede BBQ Badass Texas Boost or your favorite SPG rub on all sides. Then smear the herb paste all over the leg of lamb. Marinate in the refrigerator for at least four hours but preferably overnight.

3. Set the smoker or grill to 325°F or 163°C. Use oak wood for flavor if using wood or pellets.

4. Roast the leg of lamb in the grill until it reaches an inner temperature of 130°F or 54°C, this will take about two hours or so.

5. When the leg of lamb is done cooking, remove it from the grill and place in an aluminum pan. Put a couple of slices of butter on top, cover with foil and let the lamb rest for at least 15 minutes.

6. When rested, remove from aluminum pan and slice against the grain. Serve immediately.

LAMB CHOPS

INGREDIENTS

- 2 racks Lamb Rib Loin
- Big Swede BBQ Badass Beef Boost
- 1 Lemon

SERVES
4–6

TIME
10 MINS

METHOD
GRILLING

METHOD

1. Trim extra fat from the lamb racks and then slice the racks into individual chops.

2. Season each lamb chop with the Big Swede BBQ Badass Beef Boost or your favorite beef rub and let sit for 60 minutes in room temperature to allow the rub to adhere to the lamb.

3. Light or set your grill to direct grilling 600°F or 315°C. If using wood or pellets, use oak or hickory wood. Let the grates get hot for at least 10 minutes.

4. Place the lamb chops on the grill and grill for 3–4 minutes. Then flip over and continue grill until cooked through, with an inner temperature of 130°F or 54°C. Lamb chops are fatty cuts so move around the lamb chops on the grill to avoid flare-ups that might char the lamb chops and make them taste bitter.

5. When almost ready, slice the lemon in half and squeeze some lemon juice on top of the chops. Remove from the grill.

6. Let the grilled lamb chops rest for 5 minutes then serve immediately.

600°F or 315°C
10 MINS

INGREDIENTS

- 1 Whole Rabbit
- Big Swede BBQ Badass Texas Boost
- 2 Tbs Butter, unsalted
- 1 Yellow Onion, chopped
- 4 Tbs Garlic, minced
- ½ lb Pork Chorizo
- 1 cup Port Wine
- 1 Tbs Worchestershire Sauce
- 2 Roma Tomatoes, chopped
- 1/2 Tbs Thyme, finely chopped
- 1 tsp Cloves
- 1 tsp Celery Seeds
- 1 tsp Cayenne Pepper
- 2 ½ oz Dark Chocolate, finely chopped
- 2 Tbs Flour
- 4 cups Chicken Stock
- Salt and Pepper, to taste

Spanish Rabbit Stew with
CHOCOLATE

SERVES	TIME	METHOD
3-4	90 MINS	GRILLING AND BRAISING

Grilled rabbit covered with an unctuous chocolate sauce is comfort food for chilly evenings

METHOD

1. Remove the innards and trim the rabbit into 6 pieces. Remove any silverskin and excess chunks of fat.

2. Season the rabbit pieces with the Big Swede BBQ Badass Texas Boost or your favorite SPG rub and let it sit for at least 15 minutes to infuse flavors.

3. Light or set your grill to 600°F or 315°C. If using wood, use oak or hickory wood. Let the grates get hot for at least 10 minutes.

4. Grill the rabbit pieces until every piece have a nice char. They do not have to be cooked through, they only need to have a caramelized surface with a light char.

5. Place a heavy cast iron skillet on the grill and melt the butter. Add onion and cook for a minute. Add garlic and cook for another minute.

Then add the chorizo and cook until chorizo is browned.

6. Next, add the port wine and let it reduce to half. Add the tomatoes and stir. Then add cloves, thyme, celery seeds and cayenne pepper and stir. Next, add chocolate and flour and stir gently.

7. Add chicken stock and let reduce to 3/4. Add the grilled rabbit parts.

8. Lower the temperature on the grill to 350°F or 177°C and simmer the stew for at least an hour or until the rabbit is tender and cooked through.

9. When the stew has a good consistency and the rabbits are done, season the stew with salt and black pepper to taste.

10. Serve the rabbit stew with rice or potatoes and a bold Rioja wine.

Blackberry Sauce and
ELK TENDERLOINS

SERVES 3-4   **TIME 60 MINS**   **METHOD SMOKING**

INGREDIENTS

- 1 lb Elk Tenderloin
- Big Swede BBQ Badass Texas Boost
- 2 Tbs Butter, unsalted
- 2 Shallots, finely chopped
- 1 cup Blackberries
- 1 Tbs Red Currant Jelly
- 1 Tbs Thyme, finely chopped
- 2 Tbs Brandy
- 3/4 cup Beef Stock, concentrated
- Salt and Pepper, to taste
- 4 Tbs Butter, sliced

**225°F, 107°C
60 MINS**

METHOD

1. Trim the elk tenderloins and remove any silverskin and excess fat. Season the tenderloins with the Big Swede BBQ Badass Texas Boost or your favorite SPG rub. Let them sit for at least an hour to allow the seasoning to adhere with the meat.

2. Set your grill or smoker to 225°F or 107°C. If using wood or pellets, use hickory wood.

3. Place the elk tenderloins in the smoker and smoke until they reach an inner temperature of 115°F or 46°C.

4. While the elk tenderloins are smoking, melt the butter in a sauce pan over high heat. Add the shallots and cook until translucent.

5. Add the blackberries, red currant and thyme and cook for two more minutes,

6. Add the brandy and the beef stock and let reduce until you have a syrupy texture, about 6-8 minutes.

7. Season the blackberry sauce with salt and pepper to taste and keep warm.

8. When ready, remove the elk tenderloins from the grill and increase the temperature of the grill to 600°C or 315°C. While the grill is getting up to temperature, let the tenderloins rest under some aluminum foil with a few slices of butter.

9. When the grillgrates are hot, sear the tenderloins on all sides for a couple of minutes or until they reach an inner temperature of 130°F or 54°C. Remove from grill and serve immediately with the blackberry sauce.

Wild Boar
MEATBALLS

SERVES	TIME	METHOD
4-6	65 MINS	SMOKING

INGREDIENTS

- 1 lb Ground Wild Boar
- 1 Egg
- 1/2 cup Bread Crumbs
- 1 Tbs Big Swede BBQ Badass Burger Boost
- 1/2 Tbs Rosemary, finely chopped
- 1/2 Tbs Sage, finely chopped
- 1/2 Tbs Thyme, finely chopped
- 1 Tbs Juniper Berries, minced
- 2 Tbs Pork Lard
- 2 Tbs Butter
- 3 Garlic Cloves
- Sprigs of Thyme and Rosemary

Sweet Chili Dressing:
- 2 cups Sheep Milk Yoghurt
- 2 Tbs Sweet Chili Sauce
- 1 Tbs Hot Sauce
- 1 Tbs Big Swede BBQ Badass Veggie Boost

METHOD

1. Mix the ground wild boar meat with the egg, breadcrumbs, herbs, juniper, pork lard and the Big Swede BBQ Badass Burger Boost or your favorite umami seasoning. Shape into small meatballs.

2. Set your grill or smoker to 225°F or 107°C. If using wood or pellets, use oak wood.

3. Place the meatballs in the smoker on an elevated rack and smoke until the meatballs reach an inner temperature of 160°F or 71°C, about 60 minutes.

4. Mix all the ingredients in the Sweet Chili dressing together and set aside.

5. Melt the butter in a large skillet over high heat. Crush the garlic cloves and add to the skillet. Also add the sprigs of rosemary and thyme to the skillet.

6. Add the smoked wild boar meatballs and brown these for 2 minutes in the pan.

7. Remove the meatballs from the pan and serve immediately with the sweet chili dressing.

VENISON SLIDERS

SERVES	TIME	METHOD
6–8	10 HRS	BRAISING

INGREDIENTS

- 3 lbs Venison Roast
- 1 Onion, sliced
- 2 Tbs Big Swede BBQ Badass Burger Boost
- 4 cups Beef Stock
- 1 cup BBQ Sauce
- 1/2 can Chipotle Peppers in Adobo Sauce
- 8 Brioche Buns

METHOD

1. Remove any silverskin from the venison roast and cube the roast into large chunks

2. Place the sliced onion in the bottom of a cast iron pan and then add the chunks of venison. Cover with the beef broth and the chipotle peppers in adobo sauce. Add your favorite commercial BBQ sauce to the pan. Also add the Big Swede BBQ Badass Burger Boost or your favorite umami seasoning.

3. Set your smoker or grill to 190°F or 88°C. If using wood or pellets, use apple or cherry wood.

4. Now smoke the venison in the cast iron pan for two hours uncovered. Stir every hour.

5. After two hours, cover the pan with the lid and continue to cook for another 7 hours or until the venison easily falls apart.

6. Remove the pan from the grill and place all the venison pieces in an aluminum pan and shred with two forks. Cover with foil and keep warm.

7. Pour the liquid into a sieve and separate the peppers and the onion from the liquid. Discard the solids and pour the liquid into a large skillet.

8. Reduce the liquid over medium heat until it reaches a saucy texture, about 30 minutes.

9. Pour the reduced braising liquid into the pulled venison meat and mix thoroughly. Place a healthy scoop of venison on a brioche bun and serve immediately.

190°F, 88°C
10 HRS

Grilled
RABBIT BURGERS

SERVES
4-6

TIME
80 MINS

METHOD
GRILLING

METHOD

1. Mix the rabbit, pork fat, thyme, sage and the Big Swede BBQ Badass Veggie Boost or your favorite herb seasoning together in a big bowl. Form nice round 1-inch thick burger patties. Season the patties with additional Badass Veggie Boost.

2. Mix all the ingredients for the blue cheese sauce together in a bowl. Keep cool and set aside.

3. Light or set your grill to direct grilling 400°F or 204°C. Lay the bacon slices on a baking rack over an aluminum pan and bake until the bacon is nice and crispy, about 20 minutes. Remove from grill and drain on paper towels. Save 2 Tbs of the bacon grease for later.

4. Add the bacon grease to a large skillet over medium heat, then add the thinly sliced onions and stir around to coat with the bacon grease. Slowly cook for an hour while stirring frequently. Deglaze the pan with the 2 Tbs of the balsamic vinegar. Add the rest

of the balsamic vinegar, the brown sugar, and the Big Swede BBQ Badass Texas Boost or your favorite SPG rub. Cook until a thick glaze forms, around 5 minutes. Add the onion mixture and bacon to a food processor and pulse. Set aside.

5. Increase the heat on the grill to 600°F or 315°C. Spray the grill grates with some vegetable oil.

6. Grill the rabbit burger patties until they reach an inner temperature of of 145°F or 63°C, about 8 minutes. Flip the burger halfway through the cook. Quickly grill the brioche buns to get some char as well.

7. Build the rabbit burger by adding a healthy dollop of the smoked bacon jam and the rabbit patty on top of that. Place a tomato slice on top of the patty and then drizzle with some blue cheese sauce. Add the top bun and serve immediately.

INGREDIENTS

- 1 lb Ground Rabbit
- 1/2 lb Ground Pork Fat
- 1 Tbs Thyme, chopped
- 1 Tbs Sage, chopped
- 2 Tbs Big Swede BBQ Badass Veg Boost
- 1 Tomato, sliced
- Vegetable Oil

Smoked Bacon Jam:
- 1 1/2 lbs Bacon
- 2 Sweet Yellow Onions, sliced
- 2/3 cup Balsamic Vinegar
- 1/2 cup Brown Sugar
- 1 Tbs Big Swede BBQ Badass Texa Boost

Blue Cheese Sauce:
- 1 cup Crème Fraiche
- 4 oz Blue Cheese, crumbled
- 1/2 Tbs Lemon Juice
- Salt and Pepper, to taste

Smoked Rabbit
MEATBALL SUB

SERVES
4-6

TIME
1 HR

METHOD
SMOKING

INGREDIENTS

- 1 lbs Ground Rabbit
- 1/2 lb Ground Pork Fat
- 1 Tbs Big Swede BBQ Badass Burger Boost
- 1 Egg
- 1/2 cup Bread Crumbs
- 3/4 cup Parmesan Cheese
- 1/4 cup Italian Parsley, chopped
- 3 cups Marinara Sauce
- 2 cups Mozzarella Cheese
- 4 Sub Rolls
- 2 Tbs Butter
- Parsley for garnish

METHOD

1. Mix ground rabbit, ground pork lard, breadcrumbs, fresh parsley, egg, parmesan cheese, and the Big Swede BBQ Badass Burger Boost or your favorite umami seasoning in a bowl.

2. Roll the meatball mixture into large balls, depending on the desired size.

3. Light or set your grill to 275°F or 135°C. If using wood or pellets, use oak wood. Place the rabbit meatballs in the grill and smoke for 45 minutes or until they get an inner temperature of 145°F or 63°C.

4. Heat up the marinara sauce in a cast iron pan and when the meatballs are ready, place them in the pan and let them infuse in the grill for another 10 minutes.

5. Increase the heat on the grill to 600°F or 315°C. Spray the grates with some vegetable oil.

6. Cut bread in half, making sure not to cut all the way through. Spread butter over both sides of the bread. Grill the bread butter side down until you get nice grillmarks about 90 seconds. Remove the bread from the grill.

7. Place the bread on an elevated baking rack. Place the smoked rabbit meatballs with the sauce onto the bread. Cover with plenty of mozzarella cheese. Return to the grill and cook until the cheese is melted, about 2 minutes. Top with fresh Italian parsley and serve immediately with extra sauce on the side for dipping.

INGREDIENTS

- 1 Venison Rib Loin
- Big Swede BBQ Badass Texas Boost
- 4 sprigs Rosemary
- 2 Tbs Butter, unsalted
- 1 Carrot, chopped
- 1 Onion, chopped
- 1 Leek, sliced
- 4 cups Beef Broth
- 11 Tbs Big Swede BBQ Badass Burger Boost
- 1 cup Red Wine
- 3 Tbs Red Currant Jelly
- 1 cup Heavy Cream
- Salt and Pepper, to taste

Red Currant Sauce and

VENISON ROAST

SERVES   **TIME**   **METHOD**
2–4   90 MIN   SMOKING

METHOD

1. Trim the venison roast from any silverskin or excess fat. Use butcher twine and tie it up in a nice log. Season on all sides with the Big Swede BBQ Badass Texas Boost or your favorite SPG rub. Let it sit with the seasoning in room temperature for 45 minutes.

2. Melt the butter in a large skillet over medium-high heat and brown the roast on all sides. Remove from the skillet and insert the rosemary sprigs through the butcher twine.

3. Add the carrot, onion, leek, beef broth, red wine and the Big Swede BBQ Badass Burger Boost or your favorite umami seasoning to a roasting pan. Place the venison roast on a grate above the pan.

4. Set your smoker or grill to 250°F or 121°C. If using wood or pellets, use oak or hickory wood. Place the roasting pan in the smoker. Smoke the venison roast until it reaches an inner temperature of 134°F or 57°C. Don't overcook it

because it will be dry.

5. Remove the venison from the roasting pan and let it rest under some aluminum foil for 15 minutes.

6. Sieve the roasting liquid into a large saucepan and bring to a simmer. Reduce to 1/3.

7. Add the red currant jelly and simmer for another 3 minutes or until the red currant jelly is completely dissolved.

8. Add the heavy cream and reduce the sauce until it has the consistency of coating the back of a spoon

9. Season with salt and pepper to taste.

10. Cut the butcher twine and remove the rosemary sprigs. Slice the venison roast into thin slices and serve immediately with the red currant sauce.

INGREDIENTS

- 2 lbs Venison Stew Meat
- 1 Onion, roughly chopped
- 4 Carrots, sliced
- 8 slices Bacon, finely chopped
- Big Swede BBQ Badass Beef Boost
- 2 Tbs Butter
- 1 Tbs Garlic, minced
- 3 Tbs Brandy
- 2 cups Red Wine
- 2 cups Beef Broth
- 1 lb Mushrooms, quartered
- Big Swede BBQ Badass Veggie Boost
- 1 cup Pearl Onions, peeled
- 2 Tbs Cornstarch
- 2 Tbs Red Currant Jelly
- Salt and Pepper, to taste
- Parsley for garnish

Smoked Venison
BOURGUIGNON

SERVES | **TIME** | **METHOD**
4-6 | 3 HRS | SMOKING

This amazingly flavorful venison bourguignon might even be better the following day

METHOD

1. Set your grill or smoker to 450°F or 232°C. If you are using wood or pellets, use oak or hickory wood.

2. Trim the venison stew meat and remove any silverskin or tough fat. Cut into 1-inch cubes and season generously with the Big Swede BBQ Badass Beef Boost or your favorite game seasoning.

3. Place a heavy cast iron pan in the grill and add the butter. When melted, add the bacon and cook until browned, for about 5 minutes, and then remove the bacon from the pan.

4. Add the mushrooms to the pan and cook until browned. Season with the Big Swede BBQ Badass Veggie Boost or your favorite herb seasoning and remove from pan. Set aside for later. Add the pearl onions to the pan and sauté until slightly brown, 2-3 minutes. Remove from pan and set aside.

5. Add the venison meat to the pan and brown for 5 minutes as

well. Work in batches if needed. Remove the meat from the pan.

6. Add the onion and the carrots to the pan and cook for 3 minutes. Add the minced garlic and cook for another minute.

7. Deglaze the pan with the brandy and scrape the bottom. Add the bacon and the venison meat to the pan. Cover with the beef broth and the red wine.

8. Lower the temperature on the grill to 300°F or 149°C and simmer covered for 2 hours. Add more broth if needed. Stir every 30 minutes.

9. Add the mushrooms and the pearl onions into the pan. Also add the cornstarch and the red currant jelly and stir until dissolved. Season with salt and pepper to taste.

10. Stir and cook uncovered for 40 minutes and then remove from grill. Garnish with parsley and serve immediately.

INGREDIENTS

- 4 Lamb Shanks
- Big Swede BBQ Badass Beef Boost
- 3 Tbs Rosemary, chopped
- 3 Tbs Thyme, chopped

Braising liquid:
- 4 cups Beef Broth
- 2 cups Dark Stout Beer
- 1 Tbs Big Swede BBQ Badass Burger Boost
- 2 sprigs Rosemary
- 2 Tbs Tomato Paste
- 1 Tbs Soy Sauce
- 1 Tbs Worcestershire Sauce

Smoked and Braised

LAMB SHANKS

SERVES	TIME	METHOD
2–4	5 HRS	SMOKING

METHOD

1. Set your smoker or grill to 235°F or 113°C. If using wood or pellets, use white oak or mesquite.

2. Start by trimming the silverskin and any excess fat from the lamb shanks.

3. Coat the lamb shank with a heavy coating of the Big Swede BBQ Badass Beef Boost or your favorite beef BBQ rub, then add a second layer of the chopped rosemary and the thyme. Let the lamb shanks sit at room temperature for an hour to allow the seasoning to set.

4. Mix the ingredients for the braising liquid and pour into an aluminum pan.

5. Place the lamb shanks in the grill on the middle rack fat-side down and slide the aluminum pan with braising liquid underneath. Smoke the lamb shanks until they reach an internal temperature of 170°F or 77°C, about 4 hours.

6. Remove the lamb shanks from the rack and place them in the aluminum pan with the braising liquid. If needed, add a little bit more beef broth. Cover the aluminum pan with foil.

7. Place the pan back in the grill and cook until the lamb shanks reach an internal temperature of 204°F or 95°C. Test doneness by trying to pull off some meat of the bone, it should fall off without any resistance.

8. Remove the pan from grill, lift out the lamb shanks carefully and wrap them in some aluminum foil and let rest for 30 minutes.

9. Reduce the braising liquid until it reaches a good saucy texture.

10. Serve the lamb shanks with some mashed potatoes and spoon the braising sauce on top.

INGREDIENTS

- 3 lbs Ground Kangaroo
- 2 Tbs Butter
- 2 Tbs Big Swede BBQ Badass Beef Boost
- 2 cups Tomato Sauce
- 1 liter Beef Broth
- 1 cup of Dark Stout Beer
- 1 Tbs Soy Sauce
- 1 Tbs Worcestershire Sauce
- 1 Tbs Vegemite

1st Round of Spices:
- 2 Tbs Onion Powder
- 1 Tbs Paprika
- 1 Tbs Chicken Bouillon Powder
- 1 Tbs Beef Bouillon Powder
- 1 Tbs New Mexico Chile
- 1 Tbs Chile de Arbol

2nd Round of Spices:
- 2 Tbs Cumin
- 1 Tbs MSG
- 1 Tbs Garlic Powder
- 1 Tbs New Mexico Chile
- 1 Tbs Chile de Arbol

3rd Round of Spices:
- 1 Tbs New Mexico Chile
- 1 Tbs Chile de Arbol
- 2 tsp Cumin
- 2 tsp Onion Powder
- 2 tsp Garlic Powder

4th Round of Spices:
- 1 Tbs New Mexico Chile
- 2 tsp Cumin
- 1 tsp Garlic Powder

Kangaroo CHILI

SERVES
4–6

TIME
25 MINUTES

METHOD
GRILLING

Smoking this chili over mesquite wood adds depth and complexity to it. This is also my go-to recipe when I make brisket or chuck chili. Feel free to experiment with using other chiles as well.

METHOD

2. Set up your grill or smoker to 450°F or 232°C. If using wood or pellets, use mesquite wood.

2. Place a large cast iron pan in the grill and melt the butter. Add the ground kangaroo meat. Cook the meat until browned, about 5–8 minutes.

3. Add the Big Swede BBQ Badass Beef Boost or your favorite beef rub and cook for 2 minutes.

4. Add the tomato sauce, 2 cups of the beef broth and the beer to the pan. Cook for 5 minutes.

5. Add the first round of spices to the cast iron pan and stir. Cook for 15 minutes.

6. Add the second round of spices to the cast iron pan and stir. Add one cup of beef broth, the soy sauce and the Worcestershire sauce as well. Cook for 20 minutes.

7. Add the third round of spices to the cast iron pan and stir. Add the last cup of beef broth. Cook for 10 minutes.

8. Add the fourth round of spices and the vegemite to the cast iron pan and stir. If needed, add some water as well. Cook for 15 minutes.

9. Remove the chili from the grill and serve with some raw onions and grated cheese.

Side Dishes

I believe side dishes are as important as the protein they support. Even calling them sides or side dishes diminishes their importance in a meal. A side dish can break or make any dinner. So maybe we have to rethink the term side dish. Maybe we should call them complementing, enhancement, or enrichment dishes instead.

There are so many different kinds of side dishes too, so how do you choose which one to pair with your protein?

I think the first thing to consider is color and texture. A great dish has a variety of colors and textures that complement and elevate each other.

Then we need to balance the flavors. If you have a spicy and bold jerk chicken, you don't want a spicy side dish, you want something light or creamy to balance out the heat.

The last thing to consider is the way you cook the side dish. When cooking in the backyard you don't want four recipes that all require a lot of time in the grill or the smoker. You certainly don't want four dishes that all require last-minute work.

In this section, you will find my favorite enrichment dishes. I hope you'll find your favorite too.

IDES

INGREDIENTS

- 3 Romaine Hearts
- Canola Oil Spray
- Big Swede BBQ Badass Veggie Boost
- 4 slices Bacon
- Big Swede BBQ Badass Pork Boost
- 1 cup Parmesan Cheese, shaved

Homemade Caesar Dressing:
- 6 Anchovy Fillets packed in oil, drained
- 1 Garlic Clove, minced
- 2 Egg Yolks
- 2 Tbs Lemon Juice
- 1 tsp Dijon Mustard
- 2 Tbs Extra Virgin Olive Oil
- 1/2 cup Vegetable Oil
- 4 Tbs Parmesan Cheese, grated
- Dash of Tabasco Sauce
- Dash of Worcestershire Sauce

Grilled Romaine
CAESAR

SERVES	TIME	METHOD
6-12	30 MINS	GRILLING

A grilled Caesar Salad served on Romaine Hearts makes for a fun side dish, perfect for warm summer days.

METHOD

1. Set your grill or smoker to 375°F or 190°C. If you are using wood or pellets, use maple wood.

2. Season the bacon slices on both sides with the Big Swede BBQ Badass Pork Boost or your favorite sweet BBQ rub. Place the slices on an elevated rack and smoke until crispy, about 15-20 minutes. Remove from grill and let cool. When cool, break into bacon bits and set aside.

3. Chop anchovy fillets, garlic, and pinch of salt. Use the side of a knife blade to mash into a paste, then scrape into a medium bowl. Whisk in the egg yolks, lemon juice, and Dijon mustard. Add Tabasco and Worcestershire sauce and start whisking.

4. Gradually whisk in the vegetable oil, and then the olive oil and whisk until dressing is thick and glossy. Add finely grated Parmesan cheese and season with salt, pepper, and more lemon juice if desired. Store in the fridge until ready to serve.

5. Increase the temperature on the grill to 650°F or 343°C. Make sure that the grates are scorching hot.

6. Cut the romaine hearts in halves, rinse and dry. Brush the inside of the hearts with the canola oil and season with the Big Swede BBQ Badass Veggie Boost or your favorite veggie herb seasoning.

7. Place the romaine hearts cut-side down on the grates and grill for 1-2 minutes until you have visible grill marks. Do not overcook the romaine hearts, they only need some charring Let the romaine hearts cool down and drizzle with Caesar dressing and sprinkle bacon.

8. Add shaved parmesan and serve immediately.

Smoked
HASSELBACKSPOTATOES

SERVES
4-6

TIME
70 MINS

METHOD
BAKING

METHOD

1. Melt the ghee over medium heat and mix with the Big Swede BBQ Badass Veggie Boost or your favorite veggie herb seasoning.

2. Scrub and clean the russet potatoes and then place the potatoes between the handles of 2 wooden spoons. Make incisions across each potato about 1/8 of an inch apart with a knife stopping the knife when it reaches the spoon. Make sure not to cut all the way through.

3. Place sliced potatoes on a large aluminum pan. Salt each potato both on the outside and inside the incisions as well. Generously brush each potato with the ghee seasoning mix.

4. Set your grill or smoker to 425°F or 218°C. Insert the aluminum pan in the grill and bake for 30 minutes.

5. After 30 minutes, baste the potatoes every 5 minutes with the ghee mix for another 30 minutes.

6. When the potatoes are getting soft, sprinkle heavily with the parmesan cheese and keep baking until the parmesan cheese is melted. Season lightly with black pepper as well.

7. Remove from the grill and serve immediately.

INGREDIENTS

- 2 lbs Russet Potatoes
- 1 Tbs Sea Salt
- 1/2 cup Ghee
- 2 Tbs Big Swede BBQ Badass Veggie Boost
- 1 cup Parmesan Cheese
- Black Pepper, to taste

Date Mint Tahini and Roasted
CAULIFLOWER

SERVES	TIME	METHOD
4-6	15 MINS	ROASTING

INGREDIENTS

- 9 oz Tahini
- 10 Medjool Dates
- 1/2 cup Heavy Cream
- 5 Mint Leaves
- 3 Cauliflower Heads (yellow, purple and white for nice colors
- 1 cup Pistachios
- 1 bunch Dill
- 2 Tbs Olive Oil
- 2 Tbs Soy Sauce
- 1 Tbs Big Swede BBQ Badass Veggie Boost

METHOD

1. Start by pitting the medjool dates. Mix the dates with the tahini, heavy cream, and the mint leaves. Purée in a blender at high speed until it reaches a fine purée texture. Add more cream if needed. Set aside in the fridge.

2. Trim the cauliflowers into small and nice florets. In a large aluminum pan, toss the cauliflowers with the olive oil and the soy sauce. Season with the Big Swede BBQ Badass Veggie Boost or your favorite herb seasoning. Make sure that all the cauliflowers florets are coated with the oil and soy sauce mix.

3. Set your smoker or grill for indirect heat 350°F or 177°C. If using wood or pellets, use pecan or maple wood.

4. Put the pan in the oven and roast for 40-50 minutes. Stir every 10 minutes.

5. While the cauliflowers are roasting, crush the pistachios and tear the dill sprigs. Make sure that the pistachios aren't too fine in texture.

6. When the roasted cauliflowers are ready, remove the pan from the grill. Toss the roasted cauliflowers in the Tahini mix. Plate the roasted cauliflowers in small serving bowls and sprinkle with crushed pistachios and dill. Serve hot.

Homemade
GUACAMOLE

SERVES
4-6

TIME
15 MINS

METHOD
MIXING

METHOD

1. Mash the red onion, jalapeno, and salt in the molcajete until the onion and the jalapenos are releasing their oils.

2. Half and remove the pit from the ripe avocados and add the flesh to the molcajete. Mash carefully until incorporated.

3. Add the diced tomatoes and the chopped cilantro to the guacamole and stir carefully.

4. Add the seasoning salt and the Big Swede BBQ Badass Veggie Boost or your favorite herb seasoning and mix gently.

5. Squeeze fresh lime juice over mixture and mix again. Season with more salt or lime juice if needed and serve immediately.

INGREDIENTS

- 2 Avocados
- 2 Tomatoes, diced
- 1/2 Red Onion
- 1 Jalapeno, seeded and diced
- 1/2 Tbs Sea Salt
- 1/2 bunch Cilantro, chopped
- 1/2 Lime, juiced
- 2 tsp Big Swede BBQ Badass Veggie Boost
- 3 tsp Sazanador Seasoning Salt

INGREDIENTS

- 2 cups Mayonnaise
- 3 Tbs Dijon Mustard
- 2 Tbs White Distilled Vinegar
- 1 Tbs Celery Seeds
- 1/4 cup Sugar
- 2 Tbs Big Swede BBQ Badass Veggie Boost
- 16 oz Coleslaw Mix

COLESLAW

SERVES
4–6

TIME
10 MIN

METHOD
MIXING

METHOD

1. Mix together the mayonnaise and the Dijon mustard with the white distilled vinegar in a bowl.

2. Mix the coleslaw mix with the sugar and let it sit for about 1 hour. Discard any liquid in the bowl. Add the celery seeds and the Big Swede BBQ Badass Veggie Boost or your favorite herb seasoning.

3. Add the mayo mix and the coleslaw together and mix gently.

4. Keep cold in the fridge before serving.

Cedar smoked

MUSHROOMS

SERVES
4–6

TIME
15 MINS

METHOD
GRILLING

Cedar smoked mushrooms are a great sidedish for any steak or pork.

INGREDIENTS

- 1 lb Mushrooms
- 1/2 Tbs Lemon Juice
- 6 Tbs Olive Oil
- 1/2 tsp Black Pepper
- 1 tsp Thyme, chopped
- 1/2 tsp Rosemary, chopped
- 1/2 tsp Sage, chopped
- 1/2 tsp Salt
- 2 tsp Garlic
- 1 1/2 Tbs Big Swede BBQ
  Badass Burger Boost
- 1 Lemon

1 large Cedar BBQ plank

650°F, 345°C
15 MIN

METHOD

1. Soak the cedar plank in water for 1–2 hours or until completely soaked through.

2. Chop and slice the mushrooms. Mix quarters and slices for more varied presentation.

3. In a bowl, combine the mushrooms, lemon juice, olive oil, garlic, salt, pepper and chopped herbs. Toss until completely coated.

4. Add the Big Swede BBQ Badass Burger Boost or your favorite mushroom or umami seasoning and toss until mixed.

5. Place the mushrooms on the cedar plank, spreading to cover about 95% of the surface.

6. Set grill or smoker to 650°F or 345°C. If using wood or pellets, use pecan wood. Place the cedar plank with mushrooms on the grates.

7. Grill cedar plank for 12–15 minutes or until mushroom edges are golden and cooked through.

8. Have a water spritz bottle ready for any flare-ups. The cedar plank should smoke but not light on fire.

9. When the mushrooms are cooked through, remove the cedar plank from the grill. Squeeze lemon juice on top of the mushrooms and serve immediately.

Stonegrinded Sharp Cheddar
GRITS

SERVES 4-6

TIME 30 MINS

METHOD GRILLING

These are some of the creamiest, dreamiest grits on the planet. Made from stone-ground grits, they're finished with a generous heap of butter, sharp cheddar cheese, and heavy cream.

METHOD

1. Set your grill or smoker to 450°F or 232°C. If using wood or pellets, use oak or hickory.

2. Place a heavy cast iron pan on the grill and add the chicken broth to the pan. Bring the chicken broth to a boil.

3. Add the garlic and then slowly stir in the grits. Cook the grits while stirring frequently until the grits are tender, about 20 minutes.

4. Remove the pan from the heat and stir in the cheese, butter and cream.

5. Season with salt and pepper and serve immediately.

450°F, 232°C 30 MINS

INGREDIENTS

- 4 cups Chicken Broth
- 1 Garlic Clove, minced
- 1 cup Old-Fashioned Grits
- 4 oz Cheddar Cheese, extra-sharp and shredded
- 4 Tbs Butter, unsalted
- 2 Tbs Heavy Cream
- Salt and Pepper, to taste

INGREDIENTS

- 1 1/2 lb Red Beets
- 1 1/2 lb Yellow Beets
- 1 Orange
- 1 Lemon
- 1 Tbs Olive Oil
- Flaky Sea Salt
- Black Pepper

For the Kamut
- 2 cups Kamut
- 8 cups Chicken Broth

For the Grilled Veggies
- 1 Red Onion
- 2 Red Bell Peppers
- 1 Yellow Squash
- 3 Zucchinis
- Extra Virgin Olive oil
- Big Swede BBQ Badass Veggie Boost
- Chives, chopped
- Salt and Pepper, to taste
- Light Raspberry Vinaigrette
- Parmesan Cheese

Roasted Beets and

KAMUT SALAD

SERVES
4-6

TIME
120 MINS

METHOD
GRILLING

METHOD

1. Soak the Kamut overnight in a bowl of water. Drain the water before cooking.

2. Set your grill or smoker to 600°F or 315°C. If using wood or pellets, use oak wood. Let the grates get hot for at least 10 minutes.

3. Remove the green tops from 3 pounds of beets. Place the unpeeled whole beets on the grill and cover with a lid. Cook them for about 40 minutes, turning every 10 minutes or so until they are charred on all sides and a paring knife can easily pierce the beets all the way to the center.

4. Halve one orange and one lemon and cook them on the grill, turning once, until the fruit is caramelized, and the peel is charred, about 8 to 10 minutes.

5. Use tongs to take the beets off the grill, then put them in a large bowl and cover tightly with plastic wrap to let the beets steam for about 30 minutes.

6. While you are grilling the beets, pour the broth into a pan and bring to a boil. Add the soaked Kamut and reduce the heat to low. Cover the pot and let the soaked grains simmer for 45-60 minutes. The Kamut is ready when it

is chewy and tender. Drain off excess liquid and set aside.

7. Slice the onion, bell peppers, squash and zucchinis into thin strips and skewer on bamboo skewers. Drizzle the veggies with olive oil and season with the Big Swede BBQ Badass Veggie Boost or your favorite herb seasoning.

8. Grill the skewers until the veggies has a good char and are cooked through. When ready, remove from the grill.

9. After the beets have steamed, put on some latex gloves, and use a few paper towels to remove the charred outer layers of the beets.

10. Cut the beets into small wedges, then toss with a squeeze of the grilled citrus, a drizzle of olive oil, some flaky sea salt, and freshly ground black pepper.

11. Let the veggies cool off and then cut into smaller pieces. Mix the veggies and the Kamut in a bowl and pour into a serving dish. Place the grilled beets on top and top with some chives. Drizzle with the vinaigrette.

12. Grate some parmesan slices on top of the salad and serve immediately.

Smoked
POTATOES

SERVES
4-6

TIME
45 MINS

METHOD
SMOKING

Smoked Potatoes is a great side dish for any steak, pork or poultry dish

INGREDIENTS

- 1 1/2 lb Creamer Potatoes
- 1 Onion, sliced
- 1 Bell Pepper, chopped
- 1 Tbs Garlic, minced
- 2 Tbsp Extra Virgin Olive Oil
- Big Swede BBQ Badass Veggie Boost
- Sea Salt, to taste
- Parsley, for garnish

350°F, 177°C
45 MIN

METHOD

1. Clean the creamer potatoes and cut in half. Mix with the onion, bell pepper and garlic in an aluminum pan.

2. Drizzle with olive oil and season with the Big Swede BBQ Badass Veggie Boost or your favorite veggie herb seasoning.

3. Let it sit in room temperature for 60 minutes to allow all the flavors to infuse.

4. Set the temperature of the grill or smoker to 350°F or 177°C. If using wood or pellets, use oak or hickory wood.

5. Place the aluminum pan in the smoker or the grill. Stir every 15 minutes. Cook about 45 minutes or until potatoes are cooked through.

6. When ready, remove from the grill and garnish with chopped parsley. Season with sea salt to taste and serve immediately.

Grilled and Curried

CARROTS

SERVES
4-6

TIME
10 MINS

METHOD
GRILLING

Grilling carrots will release a pleasant sweetness that balances perfectly with curry and agave nectar - I like to serve these as snacks with a yoghurt dipping sauce.

METHOD

1. Bring a pan of water to a boil. Boil the peeled carrots for 3-4 minutes. Remove and pat dry.

2. Mix the olive oil with the curry powder and the Big Swede BBQ Badass Veggie Boost or your favorite veggie herb mix. Toss the carrots in the mix, make sure that the carrots are thoroughly covered. Let sit in the marinade for 45 minutes.

3. Set your grill or smoker to 600°F or 315°C. If using wood or pellets, use pecan

or maple wood. Let the grates get hot for at least 10 minutes.

4. Place the carrots on the grill and grill until charred and slightly soft to the touch, about 6-8 minutes. Avoid overcooking the carrots or they will be mushy.

5. Remove from the grill and drizzle carrots with the agave nectar. Serve immediately.

INGREDIENTS

- 2 lbs Carrots, peeled
- 3 Tbs Extra Virgin Olive Oil
- 1 1/2 Tbs Curry Powder
- 1/2 Tbs Big Swede BBQ Badass Veggie Boost
- 2 Tbs Agave Nectar

INGREDIENTS

- 3 Avocados
- 2 Tbs Extra Virgin Olive Oil
- Big Swede BBQ Badass Veggie
  Boost
- Dill sprigs

Romesco Sauce:
- 4 Roma Tomatoes
- 1 Garlic Head
- 1 Ancho Pepper,
- 1/2 Red Bell Pepper
- 1 slice Stale Bread
- 1 Tbs Hazelnuts
- 1 Tbs Almonds
- 1 tsp Salt
- 4 Tbs Extra Virgin Olive Oil
- 1 Tbs Sherry Vinegar

Grilled Avocado with
ROMESCO SAUCE

SERVES
3–4

TIME
75 MINS

METHOD
GRILLING

Homemade Romesco sauce and grilled avocado is a match made in heaven.

METHOD

1. Set your grill or smoker to 350°F or 177°C. If using wood or pellets, use maple or pecan.

2. Cut a cross in the bottom of each tomato and place them with the garlic and the peppers in an aluminum pan. Drizzle with 1 Tbs of the olive oil. Roast the garlic for 45 minutes, and the tomatoes and peppers for another 15 minutes. Remove from grill.

3. Increase the temperature in the grill or smoker to 500°F or 260°C. Insert a cast iron pan and toast the bread and the nuts for five minutes.

4. Peel the skin off the tomatoes and peppers and pop the garlic cloves out of the skin. Place the tomatoes and the peppers in a blender and blend while slowly adding the rest of the olive oil.

5. Once it is emulsified, add the toasted bread, vinegar, and the roasted cloves of garlic.

6. Finally add the nuts and blend a bit more. Romesco sauce should be a bit grainy so do not over blend.

7. Add a large cast iron pan to the grill or smoker. Halve the avocados and remove the pitt. Cut the avocado into 1-inch cubes, and drizzle with the olive oil. Season with the Big Swede BBQ Badass Veggie Boost or your favorite veggie herb seasoning.

8. Grill the avocado chunks in the cast iron pan until nicely charred. When ready remove from the grill.

9. Place the grilled avocado cubes in a bowl and pour the Romesco sauce on top. Garnish with some dill sprigs and serve immediately.

Roasted
BRUSSELS SPROUTS

SERVES
4-6

TIME
15 MINS

METHOD
GRIDDLE GRILLING

INGREDIENTS

- 1 lb Brussels Sprouts
- 3 Tbs Chicken Stock
- 2 Tbs Dijon Mustard
- 4 Tbs Wafu Dressing
- 3 strips Bacon
- 1 Tbs Big Swede BBQ Badass Veggie Booest
- Salt and Pepper

METHOD

1. Rinse the Brussel Sprouts and remove the harder outer leaves. Also remove the hard stalks at the bottom of the sprouts and then quarter the Brussel Sprouts.

2. Set your griddle to medium high temperature. Add the bacon slices to the griddle and cook until crispy. Flip every minute. When ready, remove from the griddle and let cool. When cool, chop into crispy bacon bits and set aside.

3. Leave the bacon fat on the griddle and add the Brussels Sprouts. Slowly sauté the Brussel Sprouts until they are slightly browned, make sure that

you don't burn the leaves. This will take about 4-6 minutes. When slightly browned, add the stock. Continue to cook until stock has evaporated. .

4. While the Brussel Sprouts are slowly steam-frying, mix the Dijon Mustard and the Wafu dressing together. When the Brussel Sprouts are soft and cooked through, add the Mustard-Dressing mix and stir thoroughly.

5. Make sure that the Brussels Sprouts get covered evenly. Add the Big Swede BBQ Badass Veggie Boost or your favorite herb seasoning and the bacon bits and stir. Season with salt and pepper to taste. Serve immediately.

Grilled
SHISHITO
PEPPERS

SERVES
4-6

TIME
15 MINS

METHOD
GRILLING

Grilled Shishito Peppers are naturally sweet which balances perfectly with citrusy saltiness of Ponzu Sauce

INGREDIENTS

- 1 lb Shishito Peppers
- 2 Tbs Extra Virgin Olive Oil
- 1/3 Cup Ponzu Sauce
- Bonito Flakes
- Flaky Sea salt

METHOD

1. Rinse the peppers and toss them with the olive oil. Make sure that they are evenly covered.

2. Set the grill or smoker to 650°F or 345°C. If using wood or pellets, use apple wood. Use a vegetable tray so the peppers don't fall through the grill grates.

3. Grill until the peppers are roasted and browned, about 5-6 minutes.

4. Take the peppers of the grill and toss them with the Ponzu sauce. Season with the flaky sea salt.

5. Serve immediately and sprinkle the bonito flakes on top of the peppers.

 **650°F, 345°C 6 MINS**

Grilled

VEGGIES

SERVES
4–6

TIME
10 MINS

METHOD
GRILLING

METHOD

1. Set the grill or smoker to 650°F or 345°C. If needed, use a vegetable tray so the veggies don't fall through the grill grates.

2. Slice your veggies into pieces suited for grilling. Skewer if needed.

3. Drizzle with plenty of extra virgin olive oil and toss gently.

4. Season with the Big Swede BBQ Badass Veggie Boost or your favorite veggie seasoning. Toss gently again. Let the veggies sit for 30 minute to allow the seasoning to adhere to the veggies.

5. Grill until the veggies has a nice char and are cooked through. Serve immediately.

INGREDIENTS

- Extra Virgin Olive Oil
- Big Swede BBQ Badass Veggie Boost
- Vegetables like:
  - Yellow Squash
  - Artichoke
  - Bell Pepper
  - Cauliflower
  - Asparagus
  - Beets
  - Cabbage
  - Carrot
  - Onion
  - Parsnips
  - Corn
  - Portobella Mushroom
  - Zucchini
  - Broccolini

INGREDIENTS

- 2 lbs Flank Steak
- 1 lb of Shoestring Potatoes, fried
- Cilantro Leaves, to garnish
- Lime Cilantro Crema, store bought

Carne Asada Marinade:
- 1 Yellow Onion, roughly chopped
- 1 Garlic Head
- 12 Guajillo Peppers
- 2 cups Water
- 1/2 cup Orange Juice
- 1/4 cup Achiote Paste
- 1/4 cup White Vinegar
- 1/4 cup Adobo Sauce
- 1/4 cup Kosher Salt
- 1 tsp Oregano
- 1 tsp Allspice
- 1 tsp Cumin
- 1 tsp Nutmeg
- 2 Bay leaves
- 1 cup Extra Virgin Olive Oil

Queso Blanco:
- 1 Asadero Cheese
- 4 oz Green Chilies
- 1/4 cup Heavy Cream
- 2 Tbs Yellow Onion, finely chopped
- 2 tsp Cumin
- 1/2 tsp Salt
- 1 Tbs Adobo Sauce

Guacamole:
- 1 Avocado
- 3 Tbs Tomatoes, diced
- 1 tsp Sea Salt
- 1 Tbs Red Onion
- 1 Tbs Jalapeno, seeded and diced
- 1/2 bunch Cilantro, finely chopped
- 1/2 Lime, juiced
- Salt and Pepper, to taste

Loaded Carne Asada
FRIES

SERVES
4-6

TIME
15 MINS

METHOD
GRILLING

These fries are perfect for parties and gameday celebrations

METHOD

1. Boil the Guajillo Peppers in the water for 30 minutes. Set aside to cool slightly. Transfer chiles to a blender, add 1 cup cooking liquid, and purée until smooth

2. For the Asada marinade, add 1 cup of guajillo purée in a blender. Add the garlic cloves, onion, orange juice, achiote paste, vinegar, adobo sauce and all the spices including the bay leaves. Blend until smooth. Also add the cup of olive oil while blending until the oil emulsifies.

3. Place the steak in a bowl or Ziplock bag and cover with the marinade. Set aside overnight.

4. To make the queso, put all ingredients in a double boiler and heat on medium. Cook until melted and well blended, stirring occasionally.

5. For the guacamole, mash onion, jalapenos and salt

in the molcajete. Add the avocado and carefully mash. Add tomatoes and cilantro. Squeeze fresh lime juice over mixture. Sprinkle with salt and pepper to taste. Fold together gently.

6. Set the grill or smoker to 650°F or 345°C. If using wood or pellets, use oak wood.

7. Remove the steak from the marinade and place on the grill. Cook for 4-6 minutes on each side for a medium-rare steak.

8. Remove the steak from the grill and let it rest for 5 minutes. Then slice it in into thin bitesize strips against the grain.

9. Place the fried fries at the bottom of a bowl. Season with salt. Ladle with queso and then add sliced Carne Asada. Top with guacamole, lime cilantro crema, and cilantro leaves. Serve immediately.

Tacos

When you move to a new city, state, or country, you are exposed to new flavors and new cuisines. And you are often better off because of it. I love Arizona and the huge influence the proximity to Mexico have had on our local cuisine. I have become a Taco fanatic – I love tacos. I actually think I am addicted to them.

That wasn't always the case. In Sweden, we do eat tacos. There is even this thing called Taco Fridays. Not Taco Tuesdays, but Taco Fridays. It usually means that you go to the grocery store and buy hard taco shells, taco meat mixes, ground beef, and taco dressings. Then you cook the ground meat with the mixes and serve it buffet style. You have a variety of taco fillings so everybody can build their own. And you often eat the tacos in front of the TV. Family fun time for sure but from a taco quality perspective, not so much.

And then I moved to Arizona where you have thousands of taco restaurants and in addition, you have another thousands of street taco stands. You have gourmet tacos, you have street tacos, you even have breakfast tacos (who knew that was a thing).

I am Johan and I am addicted to Tacos.

And in this section, you will find some of my favorite recipes.

ACOS

INGREDIENTS

- 2 Iberico Secretos
- Big Swede BBQ Badass Texas Boost
- 1 Pineapple
- Big Swede BBQ Badass Pork Boost
- 1 Red Onion, thinly sliced
- 1 Tbs Butter, unsalted

Street Taco Toppings:
- 6 Flour Tortillas
- 2 Avocados
- 2 cups Roasted Tomato Salsa
- 2 cups Pico de Gallo, spicy
- 1 cup Lime Cilantro Crema

Iberico Secretos
STREET TACOS

SERVES
3-6

TIME
15 MINS

METHOD
GRILLING

The Bellota or acorn diet of the freely roaming Pata Negra breed pigs in Spain, makes a rich, nutty flavoured pork that is supremely moist and the secretos might be the best cut of meat on these pigs.

METHOD

1. Trim the Iberico secretos and remove any silver skin and excess fat.

2. Season the secretos on both sides with the Big Swede BBQ Badass Texas Boost or your favorite SPG rub.

3. Set the grill or smoker to 650°F or 343°C. If using wood or pellets, use cherry wood.

4. Slice the pineapple into 1-inch thick slices. Remove the core and the outer shell with ring cutters. Season the pineapple slices on both sides with the Big Swede BBQ Badass Pork Boost or your favorite sweet BBQ rub.

5. Place a cast iron pan on the grill. When hot, add the butter and the red onion. Sauté the red onion until browned and cooked through. When finished, remove the pan from the grill.

6. Grill the pineapple slices until they have a good char

and are soft to the touch. about 6-8 minutes. Remove from the grill and cut into small chunks.

7. Place the secretos on the grill and grill for 5-6 minutes until they reach an inner temperature of 160°F or 71°C.

8. Remove the secretos from the grill and let rest for 5 minutes. When rested, slice into small and thin slices.

9. Heat up the flour tortillas on the grill for 1 minute.

10. Build the street tacos by placing a few avocado cubes on the tortillas. Then add the roasted red onion slices. Then place the grilled pineapple chunks on the tortilla. Spoon the roasted tomato salsa on top. Then, place plenty of the secretos on the tacos. Top it off with the spicy pico de gallo. Drizzle lime cilantro crema to finish the tacos. Serve immediately.

Grilled Hanger Steak
TACOS

SERVES
4–6

TIME
6 MINS

METHOD
GRILLING

INGREDIENTS

- 1 lb Hanger Steak
- 6 Flour Tortillas
- 2 cups Baby Arugula
- 1/2 cup Cilantro Leaves
- 2 Avocados
- 1 Lime
- 2 cups Roasted Salsa
- 1 cup Lime Cilantro Crema
- Sea Salt, to taste

Hanger Steak Marinade:
- 1 Garlic Head, chopped
- 1/4 Yellow Onion, chopped
- 4 Green Onions, chopped
- 1 Tbs Chipotle Chili Powder
- 1 Tbs Smoked Paprika
- 1 Tbs Black Pepper
- 2 Jalapeños
- 1/2 bunch Cilantro
- 2 cups Stout Beer
- 2 Oranges, zested and juiced
- 3 Limes, zested and juiced
- 1 Tbs Sea Salt
- 1 Tbs Sugar
- 2 Tbs Extra Virgin Olive Oil

**650°F, 345°C
6 MINS**

METHOD

1. Trim the hanger steak by removing the line of gristle in the center of the steaks and then trim the silverskin and extra fat. You will end up with two separate cuts of the hanger steak.

2. Make the steak marinade by adding all the ingredients to a blender and blitzing to a paste. Rub the marinade all over the hanger steak and leave to marinate in the fridge, covered, for at least an hour and up to 2 days.

3. Set the grill or smoker to 650°F or 345°C. If using wood or charcoal, use oak wood.

4. Once the grates are smoking hot, add the hanger steaks and grill them until they are charred on the outside and medium rare on the inside, for about 3 minutes on each side.

5. Take the steaks off the grill and leave them to rest for 5 minutes in a warm place.

6. In the meantime, grill the tortillas for about one minute and then wrap them in a clean towel to keep them warm.

7. Halve the avocados and remove the pit. Grill the avocados for a couple of minutes until nicely charred. Let cool and then cut into small chunks.

8. Slice the steak against the grain into thin slices and sprinkle with sea salt.

9. Add a few baby arugula leaves on the tortilla. Then add the grilled avocado chunks and top with a few slices of hanger steaks. Spoon over salsa and finish with cilantro leaves, a drizzle of the lime cilantro crema and a wedge of lime to serve.

Grilled Tacos Al
PASTOR

SERVES
4–6

TIME
15 MINS

METHOD
GRILLING

Marinated and grilled pork and charred pineapple is a great flavor combination for these tasty tacos

METHOD

1. Blend all the marinade ingredients together in a blender on high. Slice the pork loin into small thin slices. Dip every slice into the marinade and place the slices in a resealable plastic bag. Pour what is left of the marinade in the bag. Let this sit in the fridge for at least 4 hours, preferably overnight. Turn the bag a couple of times to distribute the marinade evenly.

2. Set your grill to 450°F or 232°C. If using wood or pellets, use fruitwood.

3. Roast the tomatillos, onion, and garlic cloves in the grill in a veggie pan for 12–15 minutes. When ready, remove from grill, and blend in a blender with the rest of the salsa ingredients until smooth. Put in a bowl and season with salt and pepper to taste.

4. Increase the temperature on your grill to 550°F or 287°C. Grill the pineapple slices until nice sear marks and softened.

5. Remove the sliced pork loin from the refrigerator and grill the meat until cooked through with a nice char. Remove from grill and cut into thin strips to serve on the tacos.

6. Heat the tortillas on the grill for a minute.

7. Add the grilled pork, the red onions, the grilled pineapple, the salsa, the lime juice and the cilantro to the tacos and serve immediately.

INGREDIENTS

- 3 lbs Pork Loin
- 15 Corn Tortillas
- 1 cup Cilantro, chopped
- 2 Red Onions, chopped
- 2 Limes, juiced
- 4 Pineapple Slices, grilled
- Salt, to taste

Tacos al Pastor Marinade:
- 1 Onion, chopped
- 5 oz Pineapple, chunks
- 4 Tbs Orange Juice
- 4 Garlic Cloves
- 3 Tbsp White Wine Vinegar
- 4 Tbsp Guajillo Chili Paste
- 2 Chipotle Peppers in Adobo Sauce
- 1 tsp Cumin
- 1 tsp Oregano
- 1 tsp Salt

Roasted Tomatillo Chipotle Sauce:
- 8 Tomatillos
- 1 Onion
- 6 Garlic Cloves
- 3 Chipotle Peppers in Adobo Sauce
- 5 Tbsp Pineapple juice
- Salt and Pepper, to taste

Red, White, and Blue
SWORDFISH TACOS

SERVES
4-6

TIME
120 MINS

METHOD
GRILLING

METHOD

1. To make the Purple Cabbage, finely shred the cabbage using a mandolin. Toss cabbage with sugar and 1 tsp of salt and allow to sit in colander for 1-2 hours. Discard any liquid. Whisk oil, lime juice, celery seeds, remaining salt, and black pepper in large bowl. Add cabbage and toss to coat. Set aside.

2. To make the Red Pico de Gallo, stir the tomatoes, red onion, cilantro, red bell peppers, lime juice, salt, and pepper together in a bowl. Refrigerate at least 3 hours before serving.

3. For the Chipotle Crema, purée mayo, chipotle pepper with sauce, cilantro, and lime juice until smooth in a blender. Season with salt and pepper.

4. Set the grill or smoker to 600°F or 315°C. If using wood pr pellets, use fruit wood. Let the grates get hot for at least 10 minutes.

5. Trim swordfish and cut inte 3/4-inch cubes. Skewer the swordfish cubes and give them a healthy dose of Big Swede BBQ Badass Texas Boost or your favorite SPG rub.

6. Grill swordfish skewers until cooked through and nicely charred – between 6-8 minutes.

7. Heat up the tortillas on the grill and start assembling the tacos.

8. Spread the chipotle crema on the tortilla and then cover with a layer of the purple cabbage slaw on top. Add a few spoons of the red Pico de Gallo. Then place plenty of grilled swordfish cubes on the top.

9. Finally, sprinkle some cotija cheese on top and drizzle with the salsa roja. Serve immediately.

INGREDIENTS

- 2 Swordfish Steaks
- Big Swede BBQ Badass Texas Boost
- Salsa Roja
- Cotija Cheese
- Blue Tortillas

Purple Cabbage Slaw:
- 1 head Purple Cabbage
- 1/4 cup Sugar
- 2 tsp Kosher Salt
- 1/2 cup Olive Oil
- 3 Tbs Lime Juice
- 1/2 tsp Celery Seeds
- Black Pepper, to taste

Red Pico de Gallo:
- 1 lbs Roma Tomatoes, chopped
- 1 Red Onion, chopped
- 1 Red Bell Pepper, chopped
- 1/2 cup Cilantro, chopped
- 2 Limes, juiced
- Salt and Pepper, to taste

Chipotle Crema:
- 1 Chipotle Peppers in Adobo Sauce
- 1 cup Mayonnaise
- 1/4cup Cilantro
- Salt and pepper, to taste

217

Grilled
DUCK TACOS

SERVES 4-6   **TIME** 30 MINS   **METHOD** GRILLING

METHOD

1. Mix the Big Swede BBQ Badass Texas Boost or your favorite SPG rub with the oregano, red pepper, chili and cumin.

2. Score the skin of the Moulard Duck Breast in a tight pattern. Be careful not to cut into the meat. Season both sides of duck breast with spice mix. Let sit for 45 minutes.

3. To make the peachy pico de gallo, combine all the ingredients in a bowl and mix together well.

4. Set the grill or smoker to direct 450°F or 232°C. If using wood or pellets, use oak wood.

5. Grill the duck breast skin until it reaches an internal temperature of 131°F or 55°C, about 20 min. Flip the duck breast frequently.

6. Cover the duck breast loosely with foil and let it rest for 5 minutes. Then slice into thin slices

7. Heat up the tortillas on the grill while the duck breast is resting.

8. Build the taco by placing some of the duck slices on the taco. Then top with avocado and the peachy pico de gallo. Garnish with some cilantro leaves and squeeze some lime juice on top. Serve immediately.

INGREDIENTS

- 1 Moulard Duck Breast
- 6 Flour Tortillas
- 2 Avocados, cubed
- Cilantro for garnish
- 2 Tbs Big Swede BBQ Badass Texas Boost
- * 2 tsp Oregano Leaves, dried
- 1 tsp Red Pepper Flakes, crushed
- 2 tsp Chili Powder
- 1 Tbs Cumin

Peachy Pico de Gallo:
- 1/2 Red Onion, finely diced
- 2 Limes, juiced
- 1 Jalapeno, finely chopped
- 2 Roma Tomatoes, chopped
- 2 Peaches, finely chopped
- 1/2 bunch Cilantro Leaves, finely chopped
- Salt and Pepper, to taste

Baja-Style
SHRIMP TACOS

SERVES
3-6

TIME
10 MINS

METHOD
GRILLING

**600°F, 315°C
10 MIN**

INGREDIENTS

- 2 lbs Jumbo Shrimp, peeled and deveined
- 6 Flour Tortillas
- 2 Tbs Big Swede BBQ Badass Seafood Boost
- 2 Tbs Olive Oil
- 1/2 Lime, Juiced
- 2 Avocados, cubed
- 2 Heirloom Tomatos, chopped
- 1 Jalapeno Pepper, finely diced
- Cilantro Leaves, for garnish

Baja Slaw:
- 1/4 cup Mayonnaise
- 1 Tbs Crème Fraiche
- 1 tsp Hot Sauce
- 2 cups Cabbage Slaw
- Salt, to taste

Baja Sauce:
- 3 Tbs Crème Fraiche
- 3 Tbs Mayonnaise
- 2 tsp Smoky Chipotle Powder
- 1 tsp Chili Powder

METHOD

1. Mix all the ingredients for the baja slaw together in a bowl. Season with salt to taste and set aside

2. Mix all the ingredients for the baja sauce together in a bowl and set aside.

3. Mix the Big Swede BBQ Badass Seafood Boost or your favorite seafood seasoning with the olive oil and the lime juice. Toss the shrimp with the marinade and let sit in the fridge for two hours.

4. After two hours, remove the shrimp from the grill and skewer on metal skewers.

5. Set the grill or smoker to 600°F or 315°C. If using wood or pellets, use fruit wood. Let the grates get hot for at least 10 minutes.

6. Grill the shrimp until cooked through, about 7-8 minutes. Flip after 3-4 minutes. The shrimp are done with the meat is white and they have a nice char.

7. Heat the flour tortillas on the grill for 2 minutes and set aside

8. Start building the tacos by placing the baja slaw on the warm tortillas. Then add some cubed avocado and chopped tomatoes. Next place the shrimp on top of the slaw and drizzle with the baja sauce.

9. Sprinkle with some finely chopped jalapenos and cilantro leaves and serve immediately.

Grilled
LOBSTER TACOS

SERVES
4-6

TIME
10 MINS

METHOD
GRILLING

INGREDIENTS

- 3 Lobster Tails
- 1 1/2 stick Butter
- 5 Tbs Garlic, minced
- 3 Tbs Big Swede BBQ
  Badass Seafood Boost
- 2 Avocados, cubed
- 2 cups Broccoli Slaw
- 1 cup Pico de Gallo
- 1 cup Lime Cilantro Crema
- Cilantro leaves, for garnish
- 1 Lime, juiced

600°F, 315°C
10 MINS

METHOD

1. Melt the butter over high heat and add the garlic. Then add the Big Swede BBQ Badass Seafood Boost or your favorite seafood seasoning.

2. Set the grill or smoker to 600°F or 315°C. If using wood or pellets, use pecan or maple. Let the grates get hot for at least 10 minutes.

3. Cut the lobster tails in half, brush with the butter mix and place meat-side down on the grill. Grill for 3-4 minutes. Flip over and continue grilling until the lobster meat has an inner temperature of 130°F or 54°C. Baste several times with the butter mix. Remove the lobster tails from grill and when cool, cut into smaller chunks.

4. Heat the tortillas on the grill as well and then build the tacos.

5. Start by placing the broccoli slaw and the cubed avocado on the tortillas. Then add plenty of the chopped lobster meat. Sprinkle Pico de Gallo on top of the lobster meat

6. Drizzle with the crema and garnish with the cilantro. Finally squeeze some lime juice on top and serve tacos immediately.

INGREDIENTS

- 2 lbs Beef Cheeks
- Big Swede BBQ Badass Beef Boost
- 3 cups Beef Broth
- 5 Garlic Cloves, minced
- 1 2.2oz bag Lipton Beefy Onion Mix

1 white onion, quartered

- 6 Flour Tortillas
- 2 cups Salsa Verde
- 1 White Onion, chopped
- 1 bunch Cilantro, chopped
- 1 cup Cotija cheese, crumbled

222

Tacos with Smoked

BEEF CHEEKS

SERVES	TIME	METHOD
4-6	25 MINUTES	GRILLING

Smoked Beef Cheeks are incredibly tender and full of flavors. They are marbled with fat and has a richness like no other cut of beef that works perfectly for these small barbacoa street tacos.

METHOD

1. Trim any silverskin and excess fat from the beef cheeks and then season with the Big Swede BBQ Badass Beef Boost or your favorite beef rub. Allow to adhere for at least 45 minutes.

2. Set the grill or smoker to 250°F or 121°C. If using wood or pellets, use white oak wood.

3. Place the seasoned beef cheeks in the grill and smoke for 2 hours or until the internal temperature reaches around 160°F or 71°C.

4. Remove the beef cheeks form the smoker and place them in an aluminum pan. Add the beef broth, garlic and onion mix to the pan getting about an inch of liquid in

the pan. Return the pan with the beef cheeks to the grill and keep smoking for 5 hours. Flip the beef cheeks one time during the cook.

5. When the beef cheeks reach an internal temperature of 210°F or 98°C, remove the pan from the smoker.

6. Pull the beef cheeks apart and mix with the braising liquid.

7. Heat up the flour tortillas and then build the tacos. Place a large amount of smoked beef cheeks in the tacos. Add plenty of chopped white onion. Then drizzle with the salsa verde and sprinkle the cotija cheese. Lastly, garnish with some cilantro and serve immediately.

Pizzas

After World War II, a lot of Italians emigrated to Sweden to help out in the unscathed Swedish manufacturing industry, we stayed neutral in the war. And not surprisingly, in 1947, the first two pizzerias opened.

However, it wasn't until the 1970's the pizza trend really took off. Growing up, getting pizza was a fun and exotic thing we did on Fridays. We went to the local pizzeria and then you got to choose your own pizza with the very special Swedish pizza salad.

At that time, Sweden also had a lot of immigrants from Turkey, Greece, Syria, Iran, and Jugoslavia, bringing their own food culture and applying it on pizzas. So, the Swedish pizza culture is a very unique blend of food culture from many regions and that is what makes it so fun. Nothing was banned. We have pizzas with bananas and curry. The most popular pizza in Sweden is Kebabpizza. And my personal favorite is Pizza with Tenderloin and Bearnaise Sauce. Sounds weird, but it is so good.

In this section, I have mixed some classic recipes, but also some of my personal favorites. My golden rule when it comes to pizza – there are no rules. Have fun with the toppings, experiment, and find your personal favorite.

ZZAS

INGREDIENTS

- 885 grams 00 Flour
- 3 grams Instant Yeast
- 570 grams Cold Water
- 18 grams Sea Salt
- Extra Virgin Olive Oil

Neapolitan

PIZZA DOUGH

METHOD

1. Combine the flour, yeast and cold water in the bowl of a stand mixer fitted with a dough-hook attachment. Mix on the lowest speed until the dough just comes together. Let the dough rest at room temperature for 30 minutes.

2. Add the salt and then mix on medium-low for 7 to 10 minutes, until the dough is smooth and elastic.

3. Shape the dough into a tight ball, transfer the dough to a plastic bin, cover with plastic wrap, and refrigerate for at least 24 hours.

4. Gently release the dough from the bowl. Divide it into four equal portions, about 250 grams each.

5. Work with one portion of dough at a time, stretch and fold into itself with each dough piece. Using your fingers, pull the dough

under itself to make a smooth, round ball with the seams tucked into the bottom. Carefully move it in circles, taking care to prevent any tears. This will help create a tight, even ball.

6. Brush the dough balls lightly with oil and cover with plastic wrap. Let them rest at room temperature until the dough has nearly doubled in size, about 2 hours.

7. After 2 hours the dough balls are ready to be shaped into nice round Neapolitan pizzas.

8. Shape your pizzas, add the toppings and bake in a pizza oven with a stone temperature of 750°F to 900°F, or 398°C to 482°C.

Authentic
PIZZA SAUCE

INGREDIENTS

- 14 1/2 oz Tomatoes, diced with juice
- 6 oz Tomato Paste
- 1 1/2 Tbs Extra Virgin Olive Oil
- 2 Tbs Basil Leaves, chopped
- 1 1/2 tsp Oregano, dried
- 1 1/2 tsp Sugar
- 1/2 tsp Garlic, minced
- 1 1/2 tsp Kosher Salt

METHOD

1. In a medium bowl, combine the diced tomatoes, including the juice from the can, the tomato paste, olive oil, basil, oregano, sugar, garlic, and salt.

2. Whisk together so the tomatoes become soft, and everything is well incorporated. Taste and add more salt, if desired.

3. Use immediately, or store in a tightly covered container in the refrigerator for up to 5 days. Bring to room temperature before using.

Buffalo
CHICKEN PIZZA

SERVES
2-3

TIME
15 MINS

METHOD
BAKING

INGREDIENTS

- Neapolitan Pizza Dough
- 1 Rotisserie Chicken
- 2 Tbs Big Swede BBQ Badass Wing Boost
- 3/4 cup Hot Sauce
- 1 cup Blue Cheese Dressing
- 2 cups Mozzarella Cheese
- 1 Red Onion, thinly sliced
- 1 cup Blue Cheese, crumbled
- 1 cup Ranch Dressing
- 1/2 cup Chives, finely chopped

750°F, 398°C
45 MINS

METHOD

1. Start by shredding the rotisserie chicken in a bowl.

2. Add the Big Swede BBQ Badass Wing Boost or any other favorite wing seasoning. Then add the hot sauce to the bowl. Mix thoroughly and set aside.

3. Shape the pizza dough balls into nice 12-inch round thin pizzas.

4. Spread the blue cheese dressing thinly on the pizzas. Then sprinkle the pizzas with plenty of mozzarella cheese. Add the shredded buffalo chicken mix to the pizzas as well. Also add plenty of the thinly sliced red onion. Lastly, crumble blue cheese on top of the pizzas.

5. Bake the pizzas in the pizza oven for 2-3 minutes and rotate after 90 seconds. Dome the pizza and remove.

6. Drizzle the pizzas with ranch or buttermilk ranch dressing. Finish the pizzas by sprinkling the chives on top and then serve immediately.

Fennel and
SALAMI PIZZA

SERVES **TIME** **METHOD**
2-4 15 MINS BAKING

INGREDIENTS

- Neapolitan Pizza Dough
- 1 Fennel, with fronds
- 1/2 Tbs Extra Virgin Olive Oil
- 1/2 Tbs Lemon Juice
- Salt and Pepper, to taste
- Authentic Pizza Sauce
- 1 cup Provolone Cheese
- 1 cup Asiago Cheese
- 1 cup Mozzarella Cheese
- Dry Salami Slices or Nuggets
- Big Swede BBQ Badass Veggie Boost

**750°F, 398°C
45 MINSS**

METHOD

1. Remove all the fronds from the fennel and tear the fronds into small pieces.

2. Remove the bottom part of the fennel bulb, cut it into halves and remove the inner core. Also cut the stalks. Slice the fennel bulb into very thin slices using a mandolin and set aside 2/3 of the fennel slices.

3. Place the remaining 1/3 of fennel slices into a a bowl and add the fennel fronds. Also add the olive oil and the lemon juice. Season with salt and pepper to taste.

4. Shape the pizza dough balls into nice 12-inch round thin pizzas.

5. Add a thin layer of the authentic pizza sauce on the bottom of the pizzas. Top the pizzas with the cheese blend. Next, add plenty of salami nuggets or slices. Then sprinkle the pizzas with the raw fennel slices.

6. Bake the pizzas in the pizza oven for 2-3 minutes and rotate after 90 seconds. Dome the pizzas and remove.

7. Season the pizzas with the Big Swede BBQ Badass Veggie Boost or your favorite herb seasoning.

8. Finally, top the pizzas with the marinated fennel slices. Serve immediately.

Pizza with
WILD GAME

SERVES
2–4

TIME
45 MINS

METHOD
BAKING

INGREDIENTS

- Neapolitan Pizza Dough
- 1 lb Venison Steaks
- 2 Tbs Soy Sauce
- 2 Tbs Worcestershire Sauce
- 1/2 cup Extra Virgin Olive Oil
- 2 Tbs Mirin Rice Wine
- ½ Tbs Black Garlic, fermented
- 4 Tbs Butter, unsalted
- 1 cup Fresh Lingonberries
- 1 ½ Tbs White Sugar
- 1 lb Chanterelles
- Salt and Pepper, to taste
- 1/2 lb Parsnip, peeled and cubed
- 2/3 cup Heavy Cream
- 1/3 cup of Milk
- 1 cup Gruyere Cheese
- 1 cup Mozzarella Cheese
- 1 Tbs Fresh Thyme
- 1 Tbs Fresh Oregano
- 1 bunch Dandelion Leaves

**750°F, 398°C
45 MINS**

METHOD

1. Slice the venison steaks into thin slices. Mix the soy sauce, Worcestershire sauce, and olive oil into a bowl. Add rice wine and black fermented garlic. Marinate the sliced venison meat in the marinade for at least 4 hours.

2. When marinated, add 2 Tbs of butter to a sauté pan and quickly sauté the venison for about two to three minutes and then set it aside.

3. Place lingonberries in a bowl. Add the sugar and stir every 15 minutes or so for about an hour. When the sugar is completely dissolved, set aside.

4. Add a 2 Tbs of butter into a sauté pan and sauté the chanterelles until they're brown and cooked all the way through. Season them with a little bit of salt and pepper.

5. Add the peeled and cubed parsnip into a sauce pan and cover it with the heavy cream and milk.

Bring to a boil and when it's boiling, remove the lid and cook uncovered for about 15 minutes. Season with salt and pepper. When the parsnip is soft to the touch, use an immersion blender and blend until you have a smooth sauce.

6. Shape the pizza dough into nice 12-inch round thin pizza. Add a thin layer of parsnip sauce at the bottom of the pizza. Then add 50% gruyere cheese and 50% mozzarella cheese. Next, add plenty of the venison meat and chanterelles to the pizza.

7. Season the pizza with some fresh thyme and oregano. Add a handful of dandelion leaves as well.

8. Bake the pizza in the pizza oven for 2-3 minutes and rotate after 90 seconds. Dome the pizza and remove.

9. Sprinkle the pizza with the beautiful red lingonberries and then this flavorful Wild Game Pizza is ready to serve.

Whitefish
ROE PIZZA

SERVES **TIME** **METHOD**
2-3 **15 MINS** **BAKING**

The whitefish roe pizza is a luxurious delicacy that really brings me back to summers in Sweden and the fresh and natural flavors of fresh seafood.

METHOD

1. Shape the pizza dough balls into nice 12-inch round thin pizzas.

2. Sprinkle Boursin Garlic and Herb cheese or other herb-flavored cream cheese on the pizza bottom.

3. Add plenty of shredded gruyere cheese to the pizzas. You can also use a mix of mozzarella, parmesan and cheddar.

4. Bake the pizzas in the pizza oven for 2-3 minutes and rotate after 90 seconds. Dome the pizza and remove.

5. Sprinkle the pizza with the finely chopped red onion. Then add 8 dollops of the whitefish or vendace roe. The only limitation here is your wallet – vendace roe can be expensive.

6. Whisk a cup of crème fraiche to make it fluffy and airy. Add 8 dollops of the creme fraiche to the pizzas as well.

7. Finally, top the pizzas with plenty of dill sprigs and serve the whitefish roe pizzas immediately.

INGREDIENTS

- Neapolitan Pizza Dough
- 2 Boursin Garlic and Herb Cheese
- 1 cup Gruyere Cheese, shredded
- 1 Red Onion, finely chopped
- 1 cup Whitefish or Vendace Roe
- 1 cup Crème Fraiche, whipped
- Dill sprigs, to garnish

Tenderloin and Bearnaise Sauce
PIZZA

———— ● ————

SERVES
4-6

TIME
20 MINS

METHOD
BAKING

Bearnaise Sauce and Beef Tenderloin on a
pizza is awesome. Yes. It. Is.

INGREDIENTS

- **Neapolitan Pizza Dough**
- **Authentic Pizza Sauce**
- **2 cups Mozzarella Cheese**
- **1/2 lb Beef Tenderloin**
- **Big Swede BBQ Badass Beef Boost**
- **1 Tbs Butter**
- **1/2 lb White Mushrooms, sliced**
- **1 Yellow Onion, chopped**
- **2 cups Bearnaise sauce**
- **1/2 Tbs Turmeric**

METHOD

1. Cut the tenderloin into 1-inch cubes and season thoroughly with the Big Swede BBQ Badass Beef Boost or your favorite beef seasoning.

2. Melt the butter in a sautépan over medium heat and then sauté the tenderloin cubes until browned, about 10 minutes. Remove them from the pan and set aside. Sauté the mushrooms in the same pan until browned and then set aside.

3. Make or heat the bearnaise sauce. For this recipe, use Knorr Bearnaise Mix and add turmeric for some color.

4. Shape the pizza dough balls into nice 12-inch round thin pizzas.

5. Add a layer of the authentic pizza sauce on the bottom. Then add the mozzarella cheese, the tenderloin, the mushrooms and the chopped onion. Also add a few dollops of the bearnaise sauce.

6. Bake the pizzas in the pizza oven for 2-3 minutes and rotate after 90 seconds. Dome the pizzas and remove.

7. Slice the pizza and serve immediately.

Cup and Char
RONI PIZZA

SERVES	TIME	METHOD
4-6	10 MINS	BAKING

I love making Pepperoni Pizza using cup and char pepperoni. The pizzas looks amazing and the cups collect some the pepperoni grease which adds flavors but also helps reduce the greasiness.

METHOD

1. Shape the pizza dough balls into nice 12-inch round thin pizzas.

2. Add a thin layer of the authentic pizza sauce on the bottom of the pizzas. Season lightly with the Big Swede BBQ Badass Veggie Boost or your favorite herb seasoning. Top the pizzas with the mozzarella cheese and then sprinkle lightly with the parmesan cheese.

3. Place plenty of your favorite brand of cup and char pepperoni. You can of course use regular pepperoni too, but the cupped one looks so much better on the pizza.

4. Bake the pizzas in the pizza oven for 2-3 minutes and rotate after 90 seconds. Dome the pizzas and remove.

5. Slice the pizza and serve immediately.

INGREDIENTS

- Neapolitan Pizza Dough
- Authentic Pizza Sauce
- Mozzarella Cheese, shredded
- Parmesan Cheese
- Big Swede BBQ Badass Veggie Boost
- Cup & Char Spicy Pepperoni

BBQ Pizza with

PULLED PORK

SERVES
4–6

TIME
10 MINS

METHOD
BAKING

METHOD

1. Make the cilantro crema by mixing the sour cream and the dried cilantro in a bowl. Zest and juice the lime and mix thoroughly. Set aside.

2. Shape the pizza dough balls into nice 12-inch round thin pizzas.

3. Spread a layer of ricotta cheese on the pizza and then sprinkle with plenty of shredded mozzarella cheese.

4. Place pulled pork (and you can use the recipe in this book) all over the pizza. Add the thinly sliced red onion and season lightly the Big Swede BBQ Badass Veggie Boost or your favorite veggie herb seasoning.

5. Bake the pizzas in the pizza oven for 2–3 minutes and rotate after 90 seconds. Dome the pizzas and remove.

6. Drizzle the pizza with your favorite commercial or homemade BBQ sauce and then drizzle again with the cilantro crema.

7. Garnish with some fresh cilantro leaves and serve immediately.

INGREDIENTS

- Neapolitan Pizza Dough
- 2 cups Pulled Pork
- 1 Red Onion, thinly sliced
- Big Swede BBQ Badass Veggie Boost
- 2 cups Ricotta Cheese
- 2 cups Mozzarella Cheese
- 2 cups BBQ Sauce
- Cilantro Leaves, for garnish

Cilantro Crema:
- 15 oz Sour Cream
- 1 Tbs Cilantro, dry
- 1 Lime, zested and juiced

FRUTTI DI MARE

SERVES **TIME** **METHOD**
2-4 15 MINS BAKING

INGREDIENTS

- **Neapolitan Pizza Dough**
- **2 cups Authentic Pizza Sauce**
- **1 Fennel**
- **3/4 cup Heavy Cream**
- **10 Scallops**
- **Big Swede BBQ Badass Seafood Boost**
- **1 cup Mozzarella Cheese**
- **1 cup Black Mussels, cooked**
- **1 cup North Atlantic Shrimp, cooked**

750°F, 398°C
45 MINSS

METHOD

1. Remove all the fronds from the fennel and tear into small pieces.

2. Remove the bottom part of the fennel bulb, cut it into halves and remove the inner core. Also cut the stalks. Slice the fennel bulb into very thin slices using a mandolin and set aside 2/3 of the fennel slices.

3. Finely chop the remaining 1/3 of the fennel slices and place in a pan. Add the pizza sauce and heavy cream into the pan as well. Bring the pan up to boil over medium heat and simmer for 10 minutes.

4. Slice the scallops into thin slices and set aside.

5. Shape the pizza dough balls into nice 12-inch round thin pizzas.

6. Thinly spread the fennel and pizza sauce on top of the pizzas.

7. Season the pizzas with the Big Swede BBQ Badass Seafood Boost or your favorite seafood herbs. Add plenty of mozzarella cheese. Also add the scallop slices, the mussels and the shrimp. Lastly, sprinkle with shaved fennel.

8. Bake the pizza in the pizza oven for 2-3 minutes and rotate after 90 seconds. Dome the pizza and remove.

9. Finally, top the pizzas with the fennel fronds and serve immediately.

Pear, Roquefort and Jamon
WHITE PIZZA

SERVES 2-4

TIME 45 MINS

METHOD BAKING

INGREDIENTS

- Neapolitan Pizza Dough
- 1 Red Onion, Sliced
- 1 Tbs Sea Salt
- 1 Lemon
- 3 Bosc or Anjou Pears
- 2 cups Red Wine
- 1 cup Ricotta Cheese
- 1 cup Roquefort Cheese
- 1/2 cup Pine Nuts
- 5 oz Baby Arugula
- 10 slices Jamon Serrano
- Black Pepper, to taste
- 2 Tbs Extra Virgin Olive Oil

METHOD

1. Slice the red onion into thin slices and place in a bowl. Season with the sea salt. Halve the lemon and squeeze the juice into the bowl as well. Mix and set aside.

2. Peel and remove the core from the pears. Cut into quarters and thinly slice. Add the wine to a large sautépan and bring to boil. Add the pears and simmer for 5 minutes. Flip them and simmer for another 5 minutes. Remove from pan and let dry on a paper towel.

3. Shape the pizza dough into nice 12-inch round thin pizzas.

4. Spread a thin layer of ricotta cheese on top of the pizzas.

5. Place the poached pears evenly on top of the ricotta cheese.

6. Crumble plenty of roquefort cheese around the pear slices.

7. Sprinkle the pizzas with plenty of pinenuts. Use toasted pine nuts for an even deeper flavor.

8. Bake the pizza in the pizza oven for 2-3 minutes and rotate after 90 seconds. Dome the pizza and remove.

9. Place some of the lemon marinated red onion slices on the baked pizzas.

10. Place fresh and cleaned baby arugula leaves on top of the pizzas.

11. Tear the Serrano ham into smaller pieces and place on the pizzas as well. You can also use Jamon Iberico for an even richer flavor.

12. Last, season with freshly crushed black pepper and sprinkle a dash of really good extra virgin olive oil on top. Serve immediately.

750°F, 398°C
45 MINS

Pizza with Goat Cheese and
DUCK CONFIT

SERVES	TIME	METHOD
2-3	30 MINS	BAKING

INGREDIENTS

- Neapolitan Pizza Dough
- 2 Tbs Extra Virgin Olive Oil
- 2 Yellow Onions, finely sliced
- 2 cups Duck Confit
- 2 cups Fontina Cheese, shredded
- 2 cups Mozzarella Cheese
- 1 cup Sundried Tomatoes, chopped
- 2 cups Goat Cheese, crumbled
- Big Swede BBQ Badass Veggie Boost
- Balsamic Glaze

750°F, 398°C
45 MINS

METHOD

1. Pour the olive oil into a sautépan over low heat. Then add the yellow onions and sauté until caramelized, about 15 minutes. Remove from pan and set aside.

2. Increase the heat to medium and add the duck confit to the pan. Cook until duck confit is heated up and shredded. Remove from pan and set aside.

3. Shape the pizza dough balls into nice 12-inch round thin pizzas.

4. Spread the Fontina cheese on top of the pizzas Then sprinkle the pizzas with the duck confit. Add the caramelized onions to the pizzas as well. Then add some of the chopped sundried tomatoes. Lastly, crumble goat cheese on top of the pizzas and season lightly with the Big Swede BBQ Badass Veggie Boost or dried oregano.

5. Bake the pizzas in the pizza oven for 2-3 minutes, and rotate after 90 seconds. Dome the pizza and remove.

6. Drizzle the pizzas with balsamic glaze and then serve immediately.

DESS

Desserts

The dessert is the last and final impression of a dinner and an opportunity to go out with a bang. It is the exclamation point of the meal. And after eating grilled food, people often like to end the dinner on a sweeter note.

I don't have a sweet tooth myself. I don't crave desserts. When I go out to eat, I would rather eat an extra appetizer than a dessert.

But I do have a few favorites that I love to cook.

They all have a few things in common. When I eat a heavy meal, I normally want something light and fruity as a finish. So, incorporating grilled fruits in a dessert is always a good strategy that appeals to me. I think fruit is transformed when grilled, it brings out an even stronger sweetness.

Also, when you can incorporate some savory notes in all the sweetness, I personally think it balances the dish better. And bacon is perfect for this. So, whenever I can include some bacon and saltiness in the dessert, I will do that too.

Maybe I got a little sweet tooth after all...

ERTS

Grilled
PEACHES

SERVES **TIME** **METHOD**
4-6 **10 MINS** **GRILLING**

INGREDIENTS

- 5 Peaches, ripe but firm
- 1 tsp Nutmeg
- 1 tsp Big Swede BBQ Badass Pork Boost
- 2 cups Greek Yogurt, plain
- 2 Tbs Honey
- 1/2 tsp Almond Extract
- 1/3 cup Pistachios, chopped
- Cooking Spray

600°F, 315°C
10 MINS

METHOD

1. Set the grill or smoker to 600°F or 315°C. If using wood, use peach or apple wood. Let the grates get hot for at least 10 minutes.

2. Halve the peaches and remove the pitt. Sprinkle the cut side of the fruit very lightly with nutmeg and the Big Swede BBQ Badass Pork Boost or your favorite sweet BBQ rub. Coat with cooking spray.

3. Grill fruit cut-sides down, turning once, until lightly charred and softened, about 10 minutes. Remove the peaches from grill and arrange on a serving platter.

4. Meanwhile, combine the plain greek yogurt, honey and almond extract in a small bowl.

5. Spoon each peach with the yogurt mixture and sprinkle each some chopped pistachios. Serve immediately.

Apple CRISP

SERVES	TIME	METHOD
4–6	90 MINS	BAKING

The perfect ratio of buttery crisp topping baked on top of juicy and fresh apples served with a sweet vanilla ice cream

METHOD

1. Set your smoker or grill to 375°F or 190°C. If using wood or pellets, use pecan wood.

2. In a large bowl, mix all filling ingredients and toss together. Pour mixture into a 9" round cast iron skillet.

3. In another large bowl, combine the flour, oatmeal, sugars, and salt, and mix together. Add the butter and continue mixing until the mixture is crumbly and the butter crumbles are the size of peas.

4. Place the topping evenly over the apple mixture and cover with foil.

5. Place the apple crisp in the grill and bake covered for 30 minutes.

6. Remove foil, and then continue cooking in the grill for an additional 45–60 minutes, or until the mixture is bubbly and topping is crispy.

7. Serve warm with a big scoop of delicious vanilla ice cream.

**375°F (190°C)
45 MINS**

INGREDIENTS

For the Filling:
- 3 lbs Apples, peeled, cored, and cut to wedges
- 1 Orange, zested
- 1 Lemon, zested
- 1/2 Orange, juiced
- 1/2 Lemon, juiced
- 1/4 cup Granulated Sugar
- 1 tsp Cinnamon
- 1/4 tsp Ground Nutmeg

For the Topping:
- 12 Tbs Butter, cold and grated
- 1 cup Flour
- 1 cup Old-Fashioned Oats
- 1/2 cup Granulated Sugar
- 1/2 cup Brown Sugar
- 1/4 tsp Kosher Salt

- Vanilla Ice Cream, to serve

Smoked Bourbon
BREAD PUDDING

SERVES | **TIME** | **METHOD**
4-6 | 45 MINS | BAKING

Bourbon whisky and bread pudding might be the best dessert ever invented

INGREDIENTS

- 1 loaf Brioche or Challah Bread, day old
- 1/2 cup Raisins
- 1/2 cup Walnuts or pecans
- 3 Eggs
- 1/2 cup Brown Sugar
- 1 Tbs Cinnamon
- 1 1/2 tsp Nutmeg
- 1/2 tsp Ground Ginger
- 1 Tbs Vanilla Extract
- 1 cup Heavy Cream
- 1/2 cup Coffee

Bourbon Sauce:
- 16 Tbs Butter, unsalted
- 2 cups Brown Sugar
- 1 cup Bourbon Whisky

**350°F, 177°C
45 MIN**

METHOD

1. To make the bourbon sauce, start with mixing the butter and sugar together. Start heating the mixture over very low heat. Stir with a wooden spoon until the sugar is completely dissolved.

2. Add the bourbon and cook the bourbon sauce at a very, very, very low temperature for 2 hours. This maybe more sauce than you will need, but it cooks better this way. Set aside until serving.

3. Cut bread in 1-inch cubes the night before and leave out to stale. Place the bread cubes, raisins and nuts in a big bowl and toss to combine.

4. In a medium bowl, combine the sugar, spices, vanilla, cream, and coffee and whisk until mixed.

5. Pour the mixture over the bread cube mixture and let sit 1 hour in the fridge.

6. Set grill or smoker to 350°F or 177°C. If using wood or pellets, use apple or cherry wood.

7. Pour the bread pudding mix into a 2-inch deep greased baking pan and bake for 45 minutes.

8. To serve, pour the Bourbon Sauce over the bread pudding and serve immediately.

Grilled Peach
COBBLER

SERVES
4-6

TIME
40 MINS

METHOD
GRILLING

METHOD

1. Set grill or smoker to 425°F or 218°C. If using wood or pellets, use apple or cherry wood.

2. In a large bowl, add sliced peaches, lemon juice, cornstarch, brown sugar, vanilla extract, and cinnamon. Toss to combine. Pour peach mixture into cast iron skillet and bake in the grill for 10 minutes.

3. In a small mixing bowl, combine the white sugar and the cinnamon. Stir to combine and set aside.

4. In a medium mixing bowl, combine yellow cake mix, brown sugar, salt, and baking powder. Stir to combine. Add the grated butter into the mixture until it resembles coarse crumbs.

5. Once the peaches are done cooking, remove from the grill and sprinkle with the cinnamon and sugar mix. Then add the crumb topping to cover the peaches entirely.

6. Set back in the grill and bake for 25-30 minutes or until crumb topping is a nice golden brown.

7. Serve immediately with the vanilla ice cream.

INGREDIENTS

- 10 Peaches pit removed, peeled & sliced
- 2 Tbs Lemon Juice
- 2 tsp Cornstarch
- 1/2 cup Brown Sugar
- 2 tsp Vanilla Extract
- 2 tsp Cinnamon
- Vanilla Ice Cream, to serve

Crumb Topping:
- 1 1/2 cups Yellow Cake Mix
- 1/4 cup Brown Sugar
- 1 tsp Salt
- 1 tsp Baking Powder
- 8 Tbs Butter, unsalted, chilled and grated
- 2 Tbs White Sugar
- 1 tsp Cinnamon

425°F, 218°C
40 MINS

Rotisserie
PINEAPPLE

SERVES   **TIME**   **METHOD**
2-3   2 HRS   ROTISSERIE

METHOD

1. Pour the white caster sugar into a hot pan and melt while whisking constantly. When it darkens, add the butter a little at a time, whisking to emulsify. Remove from the heat, then add the salt and whisk until fully dissolved.

2. Add 1/3 of the apple juice and whisk until fully incorporated and repeat with the next 2/3 of the juice. Place back on heat and bring to the boil. Allow the basting sauce to cool.

3. Set your grill to 450°F or 232°C and set it up for rotisserie grilling. If using wood or pellets, use cherry or apple wood.

4. Remove the skin from the pineapple and slice a "trench" about 2 cm deep and 3cm wide, diagonally from top to bottom.

5. Place the pineapple on the rotisserie rod. Place an aluminum pan underneath to catch the basting sauce and prevent burning. Turn the rotisserie function on and roast for a couple of hours while basting the pineapple with the basting sauce regularly. The pineapple is ready when the basting sauce is caramelized, and the pineapple is soft and cooked through.

6. To make the caramel sauce, place the ingredients in a saucepan over a medium heat and bring to the boil. Whisk until the sauce reaches 250°F or 121°C, then remove from heat.

7. Remove the pineapple from the rotisserie rod and slice into thick slices. Serve immediately with vanilla ice cream and caramel sauce.

INGREDIENTS

- Ingredients:
- 2 cups White Caster Sugar
- 1/2 cup Butter, unsalted and cubed
- 1 1/2 tsp Salt
- 1 cup Apple Juice
- 1 Pineapple

Caramel Sauce:
- 3/4 cups Demerara Sugar
- 1/2 cup Golden Syrup
- 1/2 cup Heavy Cream

Vanilla Ice Cream, to serve

Grilled and glazed
FRUIT KABOBS

SERVES
4-6

TIME
10 MINS

METHOD
GRILLING

INGREDIENTS

- 1 Cantaloupe Melon
- 1 Pineapple
- 2 Mangoes
- 3 Kiwis
- 12 Strawberries

Badass Sweet Glaze:
- 2 Tb Butter
- 1/2 cup Apple Juice
- 1/2 cup Agave Nectar
- 2 Tbs Big Swede BBQ Badass Pork Boost

 **600°F, 315°C 10 MIN**

You can almost grill any fruits or berries using this recipe so feel free to experiment

METHOD

1. Peel, pitt and cut the melon, pineapple, mangoes and kiwis into 1-inch cubes.

2. Set the grill or smoker to 600°F or 315°C. If using wood or pellets, use fruit wood. Let the grates get hot for at least 10 minutes.

3. Skewer the fruits and the berries on wooden or metal skewers.

4. Melt the butter over medium heat and add the apple juice, agave nectar and the Big Swede BBQ Badass Pork Boost or your favorite sweet BBQ rub.

5. Brush the fruit skewers with the glaze and place on the grill.

6. Grill until fruit is heated through and has nice grill marks, about 8 minutes. Rotate and baste every two minutes with the glaze.

7. Remove the skewers from the grill and baste one final time. Serve immediately.

Grilled
BANANA BOATS

SERVES
4-6

TIME
10 MINS

METHOD
GRILLING

METHOD

1. Set the grill or smoker to 600°F or 315°C. If using wood or pellets, use fruit wood.

2. Peel the bananas, I prefer my banana boats peeled but you can keep them unpeeled as well. Make a deep lengthwise cut along the inside curve of each banana, being careful not to cut all the way through. Open the cut carefully to form pocket. Shape 1 sheet of foil around each banana, forming boats.

3. Fill the banana boats with marshmallow, chocolate chips and crushed pecans.

4. Wrap the aluminum foil around the banana boats and seal the top. Leave a small space between the top of the banana and the foil.

5. Place the foiled banana boats on the grill and grill for 10 minutes.

6. Remove from the grill, unwrap the bananas and serve immediately in the foil boats.

INGREDIENTS

- 4 Bananas, ripe and straight
- 1 cup Mini Marshmallows
- 1 cup Semi Sweet Chocolate Chips
- 1/2 cup Pecans, crushed

Bacon-Wrapped
OREO COOKIES

SERVES | **TIME** | **METHOD**
4–8 | 45 MINS | SMOKING

Bacon-Wrapped Oreo Cookies are Salty, Sweet and Delicious

METHOD

1. Set your smoker or grill to 250°F or 121°C. If using wood or pellets, use apple or cherry wood.

2. Slice each bacon slice in half and then wrap the bacon around the Oreo chocolate sandwich cookie. Just wrap one lap around the cookie with an inch overlap. Place the overlap bottom down so it will hold together the bacon slice and the cookie when smoking.

3. Season with the Big Swede BBQ Badass Pork Boost or your favorite sweet BBQ rub. Let the cookies sit for 30 minutes to allow the rub to adhere to the bacon.

4. Place the Oreos on the cooking grate. Make sure the bacon seam is underneath. Smoke for 45 minutes.

5. Remove from the smoker. Allow them to cool for 10–15 minutes and then serve immediately.

INGREDIENTS

• 1 Box Oreo Chocolate Sandwich Cookies
• 1 package Sliced Bacon
• Big Swede BBQ Badass Pork Boost

250°F, 121°C
45 MINS

Grilled Pineapple with
RASPBERRY COULIS

SERVES
4–6

TIME
15 MINS

METHOD
GRILLING

METHOD

1. Cut the top and the bottom off the pineapple and then peel and core it. Slice the pineapple into 1-inch slices.

2. Melt the butter over low heat in a saucepan. Add the honey, hot pepper and the Big Swede BBQ Badass Pork Boost or your favorite sweet BBQ rub. Stir and set aside.

3. Place pineapple in a large resealable plastic bag. Add the butter mix and seal the bag. Shake to coat evenly and marinate for at least 30 minutes, or preferably overnight.

4. Wash, dry, and chop mint leaves. In a blender purée raspberries, honey, lemon juice and mint leaves. When mixed, keep cool in the fridge.

5. Set the grill or smoker to 600°F or 315°C. If using wood or pellets, use fruit wood. Let the grates get hot for at least 10 minutes.

6. Oil the grates and then grill the marinated pineapple slices for 2 to 3 minutes per side, or until heated through and lightly charred. Baste with the marinade throughout.

7. When ready, remove the pineapple slices from the grill and let them cool for 2 minutes. Then slice them into nice chunks.

8. Place a few pineapple chunks on a plate and then drizzle with the raspberry coulis. Serve immediately with vanilla ice cream.

INGREDIENTS

- 1 Pineapple
- 1 Tbs Honey
- 8 Tbs Butter
- 1 dash Hot Sauce
- 2 Tbs Big Swede BBQ Badass Pork Boost
- Vanilla Ice Cream, to serve

Raspberry Coulis:
- 2 cups Raspberries
- 1/2 cup Honey
- 1/4 cup Mint Leaves
- 2 tbs Lemon Juice

Grilled Banana FOSTER

SERVES **TIME** **METHOD**
4–6 **15 MIN** **GRILLING**

Bananas completely change their flavor when grilled and when you add rum and fire to the mix, you are in banana heaven

INGREDIENTS

- 1/4 cup Butter
- 1 cup Brown Sugar
- 1 tsp Cinnamon
- 1/4 cup Banana Liqueur
- 1/4 cup Dark Rum
- 4 Bananas, ripe
- Vanilla Ice Cream

METHOD

1. Set your grill or smoker to 325°F or 163°C. If using wood or pellets, use maple wood.

2. Combine the butter, sugar and cinnamon in a cast iron pan and place in the grill. Cook and stir until the sugar dissolves. Stir in the banana liqueur and remove from the grill.

3. Cut the bananas in half and place on the grill. Grill flesh side down for 5 minutes and then flip over and grill for another minutes. Remove bananas from grill, peel and cut in half. Place the bananas in the cast iron pan.

4. Place the cast iron pan back in the grill and cook for 5 minutes.

5. When the banana sections soften and begin to brown, carefully add the rum. Then tip the pan slightly and ignite the rum.

6. When the flames subside, lift the bananas out of the pan and place four pieces over each portion of ice cream. Generously spoon warm sauce over the top of the ice cream and serve immediately.

Smoked Orange
CHEESE CUPS

SERVES | **TIME** | **METHOD**
4-6 | 6 MINS | GRILLING

These little cheese and orange cups are perfect appetizers or desserts with their smooth and creamy sweetness

INGREDIENTS

- 10 Phyllo Sheet Cups
- 12 oz Fromager d'Affinois Cheese
- 1 cup Sweet Orange Marmalade
- 8 oz White Chocolate
- 1 Orange, zested into thin strips

METHOD

1. Set the grill on high 350°F or 177°C. If using wood or pellets, use apple or peach wood.

2. Finely chop the white chocolate. Cut the cheese rind of the cheese and chop the cheese as well.

3. Place the phyllo sheets on a baking rack. Add a few chunks of the white chocolate in the bottom. Then add a dollop of the cheese. Top the cheese with a dollop of sweet orange marmalade or your favorite marmalade of choice. Top the cheese cups with some zested orange strips.

4. Place the baking rack in the grill or smoker for about 6 minutes or until the cheese is starting to melt.

5. Remove from the grill and serve immediately.

350°F, 177°C
6 MINS

INGREDIENTS

- 8 strips Maple Bacon
- 1 Ghirardelli's Dark Chocolate Premium Brownie Mix
- 1/2 cup Butter, salted
- 1 cup Brown Sugar
- 1/2 cup Maple Syrup

Nobody can resist a smoked brownie with sprinkled maple bacon and topped with a sticky caramelized maple glaze.

Smoked Bacon and Maple
BROWNIES

SERVES
4-6

TIME
45 MINS

METHOD
SMOKING

METHOD

1. In a frying pan over medium heat, cook bacon to desired texture. Remove from heat and transfer bacon to a paper towel lined plate to absorb excess bacon grease. When cool, break into bacon bits

2. Mix the brownie batter according to instructions and pour into a greased 8×8 inch baking pan.

3. Set your grill or smoker to 325°F or 163°C. If using wood or pellets, use maple wood.

4. Place the baking pan in smoker and bake for 35–40 minutes.

5. Meanwhile, in a small saucepan over medium heat, melt salted butter. Add brown sugar and stir until completely dissolved. Increase heat and boil for 2 minutes. Stir in maple syrup and continue to boil for another 2 minutes until thickened. Syrup is ready once it coats the back of a spoon

6. When ready, remove the baking pan from smoker and let cool for 2 minutes.

7. Top each brownie with the bacon and generously pour syrup over the brownies. Cut into squares and serve warm or at room temperature.

Grilled
S'MORES PIZZA

SERVES
4-6

TIME
8 MINS

METHOD
BAKING

METHOD

1. Set your grill or smoker to 450°F or 232°C. If using wood or pellets, use fruit wood.

2. Place crust on pizza pan or cookie sheet and bake for 5 minutes in the grill.

3. Spread a thin layer of Nutella on top of the crust. Cover crust in mini marshmallows, crumbled graham crackers and 1 cup of the chocolate chips.

4. Return the crust with the toppings to the grill and bake for 3 minutes or until marshmallows turn golden brown. Remove from the grill.

5. Sprinkle on extra graham cracker crumbs and vanilla sugar.

6. Melt remaining chocolate chips in the microwave and drizzle over the top of the pizza. Serve immediately.

INGREDIENTS

- 1 Pre-made Thin Pizza Crust
- 1 cup Nutella
- 2 cups Semisweet Chocolate Chips
- 1 cup Graham Crackers, crumbled
- 1 cup Mini Marshmallows
- Vanilla Sugar

Mint Chocolate and
GRILLED PEARS

SERVES
4-6

TIME
10 MINS

METHOD
GRILLING

I had a much simpler version of this dish growing up. After Eights melted over ovenbaked pears – still delicious though.

INGREDIENTS

- 4 Pears, ripe and soft
- 1/2 cup Heavy Cream
- 1 cup After Eights or Ghirardelli Mint Squares
- Whipped Cream, to serve
- 1 cup Walnuts, crushed

Badass Pear Glaze:
- 4 Tbs Butter
- 1/2 cup Pear Juice
- 1/2 cup Agave Nectar
- 2 Tbs Big Swede BBQ Badass Pork Boost

 **450°F, 232°C**
10 MIN

METHOD

1. Melt the butter over medium heat and add the pear juice, agave nectar and the Big Swede BBQ Badass Pork Boost or your favorite sweet BBQ rub. Reduce for 5 minutes.

2. Peel and cut the pears in half length-wise and use a melon baller to scoop out the seeds. Use a pastry brush to spread the pear glaze over the pear flesh.

3. Set the grill or smoker to 450°F or 232°C. If using wood or pellets, use fruit wood. Let the grates get hot for at least 10 minutes.

4. Grill until fruit is heated through, soft to the touch, and has nice grill marks, about 10 minutes. Rotate and baste every two minutes with the glaze.

5. Melt the heavy cream and the chocolate mints in a pan.

6. Plate by placing one pear in a pool of the chocolate cream sauce. Fill the pear with some more sauce.

7. Place a dollop of whipped cream on top of the pear and then sprinkle with the crushed walnuts. Serve immediately.

Pineapple and
PORK

SERVES
2-4

TIME
45 MINS

METHOD
SMOKING

Serving the pork in the pineapple makes for a real showstopper dessert

METHOD

1. Start by cutting the top and bottom part of pineapple and carefully trim away the outer hard parts.

2. Cut v-shaped cuts along the dots on the pineapple to create a spiraled pineapple. Be careful not to cut too deep.

3. Carefully cut out the inside of the pineapple using a long narrow knife. Try to cut as close to the exterior wall as possible without cutting through. Cut a slice off the cutout interior and use as a bottom lid. Cube the rest of the cutout in small cubes. Vacuum seal the cubes if possible. This will compress the pineapple cubes and make for a more dense texture.

4. Season the pineapple bowl on the inside and outside with the Big Swede BBQ Badass Pork Boost or your favorite sweet BBQ rub.

5. Mix the previously smoked pulled pork with your favorite sweet commercial BBQ sauce in an aluminum pan. Do not use a mustard-based or vinegar-based sauce for this recipe.

6. Set your smoker or grill to 285°F or 140°C. If using wood or pellets, use fruit wood like apples or cherry wood.

7. Place the smoked pork and pineapple in the grill and smoke for 45 minutes. When the pineapple is starting to get soft but not mushy, remove the pineapple and the pork from the grill.

8. Mix the warm pork and the vacuum-sealed pineapples cubes and carefully place in pineapple bowl.

9. Top with more pineapple cubes and BBQ sauce. Serve immediately.

INGREDIENTS

- 2 Pineapples
- Big Swede Badass Pork Boost
- 3 cups Smoked Pulled Pork
- 1 cup BBQ Sauce

ABOU

About Big Swede BBQ

I saw Big Swede BBQ as an opportunity to start a company whose purpose was to spread the joy of outdoor cooking. And we try to achieve this by teaching and educating people around the world how to cook better food outside using fire and smoke.

My philosophy is that when people come together around an open fire, a BBQ pit, or a grill, social interactions and bonds are strengthened and life, in an instant, becomes more BADASS.

I hope that our paths will meet some day and that there will be an open fire, a few beers, maybe a cigar, and some food to cook together. I am looking forward to the stories and the laughters.

Until then, here is some more information about how Big Swede BBQ came about, what kind of equipment and products we use, and of course more information about our award-winning rubs.

Thanks again for your support.

And Happy Grilling!

T   U S

THE LOVE OF FIRE

I think I inherited the passion for cooking from my parents. I grew up in Sweden in the 1970s. We were middle class. My dad was travelling every week and my mom was a stay-at-home mom. I would say we were a typical Swedish middle-class family.

Both my mom and my dad were great at cooking. But in different ways. Mom cooked the weekday meals. And in Sweden during the 1970s, that meant casseroles, stews, meatloaves, and of course Swedish Meatballs. I loved my mom's homecooking, I still do. It was simple and honest food, and it was always tasty. And I feel very blessed that after coming home from playing outdoors with my friends and starving after running around for hours, mom was always there, cooking up a homecooked meal. On the picture you can see her serve up some chocolate balls at my 6th birthday party. I am the boy with the red had and the ubercool purple shirt.

My dad was an accountant for one of the biggest commercial banks in Sweden and he was travelling most weeks. When he came home during the weekends, he took over the kitchen. We mostly ate at home, I can't really remember a lot of times during my childhood when we went out to a restaurant to eat. The only time it really happened was when my dad came home late on a Friday night and was too tired to cook. That is when we went to the local pizzeria and ordered some takeaway pizza. And what a feast that was. Pizzas in Sweden was the big thing. And still is to this day. The first thing I eat when I travel back to Sweden, is a Swedish pizza. They have an unique flavor and I can sometimes wake up in the morning and the craving for Swedish pizza is real.

But back to my dad. On Saturdays and Sundays, it was his time to cook. And my dad was a great cook. Always looking for fresh produce whether it was foraging mushrooms or berries in the woods or going to the local fishmonger and get some fresh fish or shellfish straight off the boats. We also had great access to game meat like moose, venison or elk. I never saw my dad follow a recipe. He cooked and tasted, cooked and tasted, and it always turned out amazing. His moose roast with gravy is still one of the best things I have ever eaten, and I have had the fortune of eating at some of the best restaurants in the world. Looking back at my childhood, I never thought that I would inherit this passion for cooking. Back then I was more interested in eating the food than cooking it.

But I can see that I have a little of both my mom and my dad in me when it comes to my love for food. From my mom, I have the love of feeding people, the joy you see when they taste good and honest food. And from my dad, I have the love of experimenting and testing out new flavors, cuts of meats, and cooking methods.

I also think you are influenced by the country you grew up in. In Sweden we have these cultural attitudes called the Law of Jante. These were first formulated in the form of the ten rules of Jante Law by the Danish-Norwegian author Aksel Sandemose in his satirical novel A Fugitive Crosses His Tracks.

In short, it means "Don't think that you are special". And it was real thing growing up. If the neighbor bought a new fancy car, that was frowned upon. If people went on exclusive vacations, people whispered rumors about obvious tax evasion.

And when you had guest, you served authentic and honest food, nothing extravagant. This meant that you would often take very simple and cheap ingredients and try to transform them into something tasteful. I still try to make my recipes this way, to take good ingredients and through a few simple steps make them taste amazing.

Outdoor cooking and grilling in Sweden when I grew up was a summer activity. It has changed a lot over the last couple of years but back then, when the days got longer and warmer, Swedes all over the country dusted off their rusty old grills. We lit them up using lighter fuel and charcoal and then we all grilled pre-marinated pork steaks called "Flintasteak" or Flintstone Steaks. You will find the recipe in this book. Sometimes we would grill hot dogs and sometimes on very special occasions we would grill ribeye steaks.

Ribs? Brisket? Pulled Pork? Nope, not in Sweden during the 70s and the 80s.
Big outdoor kitchen with grills, smokers, pizza ovens and burners? Nope, that didn't exist.
So, my love for outdoor cooking and grilling came later in life.

Another food influence in my life besides my parents has been my travels. I have been fortunate to have a career as a corporate trainer and I have been travelling the world since my early 20s. Every time I went to new place, I tried out their local cuisine. I think the best way to learn about cultures and other people, is to socialize and talk to people around a dining table. I have had the fortune to travel to over 90 countries on five continents and at every location i have tried the local food. It is inspiring. It influences what you cook and how you cook it. And you realize that all these countries and people have two things in common. They love food. And they all cook using fire.

So, there is a great love for local cuisine which often is very rustic, simple and very delicious. But the more I learnt about food, there was also a growing curiosity about how far you can push food and the dining experience. There are so many great and avant-garde chefs out there in the world that spend every awake hour thinking about how they can strive for food perfection or turn food into art.

So, I made an effort that every place I went to, I had to try out the local street food scene, but also find the most forward-thinking restaurant and chef. And over the years I have had the fortune to eat at many of the best restaurants in the world, And some of these experiences have been life changing for sure. The first time I tried Joël Robuchon's mashed potatoes in Paris, it changed the way you think of this normally pretty simple dish. Laughing throughout the joyful and fun dining experience at Heston Blumenthal's The Fat Duck in Bray. Getting my mind blown at Alinea in Chicago. Hanging out with Mark Best at Marque in Sydney. Eating at every Michelin star restaurant in San Sebastian during a prolonged weekend. On the picture above, we are at Martin Berasategui's restaurant. I think these experiences influenced me to try new things, to be adventurous, to include a couple of unexpected ingredients or dishes when having friends over.

As a consequence, I started collecting cookbooks as well. Reading about food is almost meditative for me. I don't even have to cook the recipes, I can just dream of the flavors when reading these recipes. And now I have written one as well. Crazy!!

When I met my wife 15 years ago, it all came together. I found the love of my life, my wonderful wife and best friend Cheryl. And I also discovered the second love of my life in outdoor cooking. Moving to Arizona from Sweden is a big change, and one of the biggest differences is the weather. When you suddenly have an opportunity to grill and make food outdoors 365 days a year it opens up a new world when it comes to cooking. Or perhaps closer to 300 days a year, during the scorching summer days, it is still nice to cook indoors.

I tried my fist smoked brisket in 2005 at Famous Dave's BBQ restaurant in Peoria and it changed my life. I fell in love with the smoky and spicy flavors. I made a commitment to myself, I am going to figure out how to cook this, and I am going to cook it well. That is how Big Swede BBQ was started. We began as a BBQ competition team and we started competing. In our first sanctioned competition, we finished 7th in Brisket and Ribs and talking those walks where extremely rewarding. But I realized pretty quickly, that I didn't have the passion for competitive BBQ. I have the utmost respect for some of my great BBQ friends for the amount of effort they invest to compete every weekend, but that was not for me. I felt that BBQ is not about who makes the best BBQ, it is about hanging out with good friends and cook food together.

So that is how the BBQ rub idea started. From the beginning it was something that I thought would be fun to have and something that I could give to my corporate clients as gifts. So, I started working on the Big Swede BBQ Badass Beef Boost.

I blended and I mixed. I cooked with the rub. And I blended and mixed some more. Over a period of 3 months I was obsessed with finding the perfect blend and one day I thought that we finally nailed it. I brought it over to my good friend Josh Dae at BBQ Island in Scottsdale and he told me that I needed to bottle this and start selling it commercially.

I reached out to my partner and manufacturer Old World Spices and Seasonings and they were able to match my blend and suddenly we had our first product on the market. Then Josh pushed me into sending it to the American Royal Best Rub on the Planet competition and against 300 of the best rubs on the market, we placed 3rd in the mild category, 4th overall with the same score as number 2 and 3.

That was the beginning for our BBQ rub line. OWS started to carry our Badass Beef Boost and suddenly it was available all throughout the US. I had to pinch myself the first time a friend sent me a picture of my rubs sitting on a shelf in a small town in Wisconsin.

And we developed our Bird Boost...and then our Veggie Boost...and then our Pork Boost. The Veggie Boost was actually my wifes idea. She is vegan for medical reasons and pushed me to create a rub specifically for grilling veggies, and it is currently one of our bestsellers.

We now have 8 rubs on the market, we have resellers in Europe, all over the US and in Australia. It has been a crazy journey and the rubs opened up new doors for us.

I met Chef Mac Kirschner when he was working at Sur La Table as a Cooking Class Instructor back in 2007. My wife doesn't like cooking so I thought that if I would bring her to some Date Night Cooking Classes, then maybe she would change her mind. It didn't change her opinion about cooking at all, rather the opposite. During one of the cooking classes, she accidentally lit her sweater on fire and only my Spiderman sense and quick reflexes prevented her from getting some horrible burns. But it did bring me a really good friend who shared my passion for cooking and teaching. After realizing that we both loved cooking and teaching other people how to cook, we began planning some cooking classes and events together.

We were very different as people. Chef Mac was the encyclopedia and technician, his knife skills were amazing. I was the one coming up with the menus and entertaining the crowds. But it worked. We started to running cooking classes together and people loved it.

We delivered sold-out cooking classes every month, we did private cooking events, and we had fun showing off some of recipes on the local morning shows.

What I didn't know, was that Chef Mac struggled with depression his whole life and one day I received a call from his ex-wife that told me that Mac had ended his life. I wish that he would have said something, or that I could have done anything for him, but I have come to the realization that the best way to honor his memory, is to keep the Big Swede BBQ journey going and share with people the things he taught me. I miss my BBQ and grilling brother every day.

We also started to get requests from BBQ grill companies to help them create content and we got our feet wet creating a recipe book for Alfresco Grills.

After finishing that project, I quickly realized that in order to spread the joy of outdoor cooking and educate more people on grilling and cooking, Big Swede BBQ had to step up our game when it came to visual content.

All our classes and events got cancelled during the pandemic, so this was a perfect time to learn photography, photo editing and video editing. Losing Mac was hard and there were moments when I felt that I didn't want to continue doing this on my own. But the visual components of creating great food content, recharged me and we have had a strong focus on creating good instructional videos with fun recipes and easy techniques. It is a always a journey to grow and evolve, but when I look back at some of our earlier videos and content we created, and compare it to what we do now, I am proud of the improvements we have made so far.

We are back to delivering cooking classes and BBQ demos. We make recipe and instructional videos for some major grill companies. We have a growing following on social media, and we have tons of video content on YouTube and TikTok. We are very fortunate and blessed. And this cookbook is the next step in spreading the joy of outdoor cooking and helping people cook badass food using the grills and smokers.

OUR PARTNERS

We are very fortunate to have great partners that support our brand and our business. These are companies with great products that we can stand behind and be proud supporting. More than that, they are companies with great people. We love working with people and companies that care about their customers and share our passion for outdoor cooking and spreading the love of BBQ and Grilling.

Old World Spices and Seasonings
We partner with the world's best manufacturer of custom blended, packaged, dry food products and seasoning for manufacturing our rubs. We are also a part of their Championship Product Line together with 150 of the best BBQ rubs in the world and they are our distributor worldwide. It is a great company to work wide, with unprecedented customer service, world-class seasoning lab, and amazing leadership and sales.
www.oldworldspices.com

Memphis Grills
Memphis Wood Fire Grills makes some of the best pellet grills on the market. They are built like tanks but are also beautifully designed. They have an open flame feature that allows authentic wood fire cooking in a pellet grill. The versatility of these grills is amazing and we cook on them on weekly basis and have never had any issues.
www.memphisgrills.com

Green Mountain Grills
GMG is a highly innovative pellet grill company with the best customer service in the grill business. It is a company that truly cares about their customer and putting the best product on the market. It is the most priceworthy pellet grill on the market, and we cook a ton of food on these grills in our cooking classes and at home. GMG Family Forever!
www.greenmountaingrills.com

WPPO LLC
We love pizza, and pizza tastes better in an authentic wood fired pizza oven. We are very fortunate to partner with WPPO who is one of the fastest-growing Wood Fired Oven Builders. The reason for their success is phenomenal products and great people with good values and big hearts. We love our WPPO Pizza Ovens, and we are also happy to call the owners good friends. Get Fired Up!!
www.wppollc.com

Alfresco Grills
Alfresco Grills makes some of the best gas grills and burners on the market. Their commercial high-end products are both extremely innovative but also the most durable on the market. The company started making commercial kitchen equipment and their consumer products are built the same way. We love cooking on the Alfresco products.
www.alfrescogrills.com

Burch Barrel

I love cooking with fire, and we are very excited about our collaboration with Burch Barrel. The Burch Barrel is a very original over-fire suspended grill, smoker and fire pit designed with versatile and functional excellence. It is a very cool design and made to be the central hub for any outdoor gathering. It also cooks like a beast!
www.burchbarrel.com

BBQ Island

It is important to have access to a well-stocked BBQ store and nobody does it better than BBQ Island in Arizona. All of their locations carry our rubs and we have done a lot of fun cooking classes together. Their staff is extremely knowledgeable not only about their products but also grilling and outdoor cooking in general. Best in class!!
www.bbqisland.com

Urban Slicer

Like I said earlier, I love pizzas. And I use Urban Slicer pizza dough and pizza sauces when I want to make some pizzas fast. Great owner and wonderful products.
www.urbanslicer.com

ACKNOWLEDGMENT

Thank you to...

My wonderful and loving wife for always supporting my crazy adventures. Without her, this book would never have happened.

My mom and dad for teaching me the value of cooking at home and for giving me a safe and wonderful childhood.

My sister and her family for just being awesome. I am so happy that we both grew up and stopped fighting.

MacMurray Kirschner for supporting me and teaching me tons of cooking tips and tricks. I miss you a lot and I hope you finally found peace from the darkness inside. I will share your parsley trick with the world. Rest in Peace, buddy!!

Josh Dae for pushing me into launching my first rub and teaching my first cooking class. You do a lot for the local BBQ community here in Arizona, you are an amazing pitmaster and without you, Big Swede BBQ wouldn't be what it is today. You have been a huge help in growing our company and I am so thankful for your friendship. You suck as a car passenger though.

Mike West, Adam, Steve, T-Bone, Chris, and everybody else at BBQ Island – you guys are the best!

Dan and Lisa at WPPO for being wonderful people and great friends. I am so happy to see your hard work paying off and thank you for including me in your wood fired family.

Tim Cleavenger and Kirtis Baxter for joining me during the early days of Big Swede BBQ. I still remember our slogan – We bleed BBQ sauce.

Our friends at Old World Spices for being an amazing business partner and wanting to take a change on Big Swede BBQ when we got started. To Amy, David, Kathy, Branden, Katie and everyone else. Thank you so much for all the hard work you do for us.

Sharla, Pam and everybody else at Memphis Grills. Working with the recipe videos has been extremely rewarding and it is so fun to look back at the first videos we made and see what enormous improvements we have made.

Jason Baker and the whole team at Green Mountain Grills. Jason, you are one of the best BBQ ambassadors I know. Thank you for all your partnership. And GMG has the best support team in the business.

Brett Edwards for being the role model and inspiration for our cooking videos. Without your support, help, and great advice, our videos would still suck like they did in the early years

Ken Gardner for being a great friend and a great ambassador for outdoor cooking as well.

Burk Forsythe for your newfound passion for BBQ photography and for helping out with a lot of the imagery in this book.

Matt Haines, Art Valentine and the whole team at Alfresco Grill and Mode Distributing. Thank you for taking a chance on us during the start of Big Swede BBQ.

All our other partners like Burch Barrel, Panhandle Milling and Urban Slices. We are honored to be associated with your brands.

All our resellers for supporting our small and family-owned business. We owe you everything and we thank you. I still have to pinch myself every day that we have resellers all across the world.

To all our local butcher shops and seamonger friends, thank you for you continuous effort of bringing the community great products. Always support your local businesses.

The BBQ community and my pitmaster friends for inspiring us every day.
The BBQ community is a caring, helpful and kind group of people with great values and big hearts. Thanks for inviting this Swede into your community with open arms.

My BBQ friends in Arizona for being the best friends a Big Swede can have. There are too many to mention, but I love you all.

Sterling Smith of Loot N' Booty BBQ for all the help over the years. It is crazy to think that two people with great BBQ rubs only live a couple of blocks from each other.

Our Swedish and European partners and customers. I love to see how outdoor cooking is exploding in Europe and I am so fortunate to have all of you as friends. And it forces me to speak Swedish on a regular basis so I don't turn into Dolph Lundgren. The struggle with Swenglish is real.

Our customers for supporting our business whether it is by using our rubs, attending our cooking classes, or just supporting us on social media. We hope that you like what we do and we are committed to improve everything we do to support you guys even more.

Connie Dowell for editing my swenglish and proofreading all these recipes.

Anders Ganten for all your tips and insights in helping me publish this book all by myself.

And to you, the reader of this cookbook. We hope you liked the recipes and that you found your favorite one. Let's bring Badass Backyard Cooking to all our neighborhoods.

OUR RUBS

Our goal with our Big Swede BBQ Badass BBQ Boosts is to make bold and flavorful rubs with a perfect balance of sweet, hot, savory and salty flavors. We want to create rubs that adds great color, great flavor and great texture to the meat it is intended for.

We want our rubs to compliment the meat and to lift the meat to new heights – not to overpower the meat. We strive to continually improve our recipes and blends and we appreciate any customer feedback.

All our rubs cater to professional chefs, competition pitmasters and backyard BBQ heroes alike.

We are very fortunate to have our rubs win several awards over the last couple of years. Our Badass Beef Boost was voted Top 3 Best BBQ Rubs on the Planet both in 2018 and 2021 by the American Royal. Our Badass Pork Boost was voted 2nd Best Pork Rub by NBBQA. All our rubs have won numerous awards on the BBQ and Steak circuit.

But the most important award for us, is the feedback we get from our customers. Nothing makes us happier that seeing posts from our customers showing how they apply our rubs in their backyard dishes.

At this moment we have a 8 rubs on the market:

• Big Swede BBQ Badass Beef Boost
• Big Swede BBQ Badass Bird Boost
• Big Swede BBQ Badass Pork Boost
• Big Swede BBQ Badass Veggie Boost
• Big Swede BBQ Badass Texas Boost
• Big Swede BBQ Badass Seafood Boost
• Big Swede BBQ Badass Burger Boost
• Big Swede BBQ Badass Wing Boost

And when you read this book, there might even be a few more.

All these rubs and seasonings are available through our website www.bigswedebbq.com

Some of these rubs are also available through our partner Old World Spices and Seasonings, please contact OWS for wholesale inquires.
www.oldworldspices.com

Follow Big Swede BBQ on Social Media for recipes, cooking tips, and updates.
We are on Facebook, Instagram, YouTube, and TikTok – just look for BigSwedeBBQ.

INDEX

CPSIA information can be obtained
at www.ICGtesting.com
Printed in the USA
LVHW070414260122
709440LV00009B/161